CW00867586

Contents

Chicken Kabobs..6

Tony's Summer Pasta 6

Blueberry Crumb Pie 7

Triple Berry Crisp 8

Crab and Shrimp Louis 8

Cauliflower Salad 9

Fettuccine with Sweet Pepper-Cayenne Sauce 10

Tomato Basil Salmon 11

Easy Peach Cobbler with Cake Mix 11

Good for You Greek Salad 12

Refreshing Cucumber Lemonade 13

Fried Soft-Shell Crab 13

Chocolate Zucchini Muffins 14

Summer Corn Salad 15

Chicken Salad with Bacon, Lettuce, and Tomato 16

Mediterranean Summer Tomatoes...16

Strawberry-Melon Summer Salad 17

Mid-Summer Italian Bread Salad..17

Tasty BBQ Corn on the Cob 18

Best Lemonade Ever..19

Grilled Pork Chops with Fresh Nectarine Salsa 19

Insalata Caprese II 20

Fresh Peach Cobbler I..21

Amelia's Tuna Macaroni Salad 22

Mom's Zucchini Bread 22

Grilled Steak Salad with Asian Dressing 23

Fresh Peach Trifle 24

Jersey Fresh Tomato Soup..25

Watermelon and Feta Salad with Arugula and Spinach...................26

Slow Cooker Lemon Garlic Chicken II 27

Strawberry Shortcake..27

Fresh Tomato Basil Sauce 28

Creamy Garlic Sauce 29

Juicy Peach Crisp 29

Blueberry Cream Muffins 30

Rosemary Ranch Chicken Kabobs 31

Grilled Beef Tenderloin with Herb-Garlic-Pepper Coating 32

Peach Muffins 32

Mexican Corn on the Cob (Elote) 33

Grilled Yellow Squash 34

Caldo de Res (Mexican Beef Soup) 34

Tomato Basil Penne Pasta 36

Greek Orzo Salad 36

Cucumbers in Sour Cream 37

Key West Chicken 38

GA Peach Pound Cake 38

Easy, Eggless Strawberry Ice Cream 39

Italian Stewed Tomatoes 40

Mom's Cucumbers 40

Zucchini Corn Fritters 41

Mexican Shrimp Cocktail 41

Salsa 42

Old-Fashioned Italian Zucchini Fritters 43

Peach Pie 44

Strawberry Angel Food Dessert 44

Old-Fashioned Italian Zucchini Fritters 45

Vinegar Pickled Carrots 46

Margaritas 46

Quick and Easy Vegetable Soup 47

Garden Tomato Salsa 47

Savory Garlic Marinated Steaks 48

Stuffed Peppers 49

Easy Zucchini Fritters 50

Easy Garlic-Lemon Scallops 51

No-Noodle Zucchini Lasagna 51

Blueberry Pie 53

Grilled Portobello with Basil Mayonnaise Sandwich 53

The Real Mojito 54

Oven-Roasted Asparagus 55

Yellow Squash Casserole 55

Microwave Corn on the Cob 56

Best Fried Green Tomatoes 57

Balsamic Bruschetta 58

Crisp Pickled Green Beans 58

Best Ever Blueberry Cobbler 59

Homemade Tomato Sauce I 60

Blackberry Pie I 61

Summer Grilled Cabbage 61

Fresh Broccoli Salad 62

Perfect Summer Fruit Salad 63

Stuffed Zucchini 63

Grilled Sea Bass 64

Garlic Chicken Stir Fry 65

Strawberry Pie II 66

Summertime Sweet Pickles 66

Tomato Mozzarella Salad 67

Easy Stuffed Zucchini 68

Red Skinned Potato Salad 69

Unbelievable Chicken 69

Fried Stuffed Squash Blossoms 70

Savory Garlic Marinated Steaks 71

Cherry Pie Filling 72

Greek Chicken 73

Burger or Hot Dog Buns 74

Rhubarb Jam 74

Fresh Tomato Salsa 75

Pesto Pasta Caprese Salad 75

Stuffed Peppers My Way 76

Connie's Zucchini "Crab" Cakes 77

Cuban Mojito 78

Enchiladas Suizas 78

Pickled Squash 79

North Carolina-Style Pulled Pork 80

Easy Cucumber Salad 82

Sauteed Cherry Tomatoes with Garlic and Basil 82

Watermelon Agua Fresca 83

Tomato, Basil, and Feta Salad 83

Thai Spicy Basil Chicken Fried Rice 84

Pineapple Coconut Zucchini Bread 85

Sean's Falafel and Cucumber Sauce 85

Key Lime Cake III 87

Chow Chow I 87

White Peach Sangria 88

Margaritas on the Rocks 89

Fried Green Tomatoes 89

Peach Upside Down Cake I 90

Simple Cucumber Soup 91

Garlic Chicken Fried Brown Rice 92

Hawaiian Chicken Kabobs 92

Summer Zucchini Casserole 93

Greek Garbanzo Bean Salad 94

Tomato Bacon Grilled Cheese 94

Microwave Bread and Butter Pickles 95

Thai Beef Salad 96

Cherry Pepper Poppers 97

Roasted Garlic Zucchini and Tomatoes 97

Jersey Fresh Stewed Tomatoes 98

Zucchini Bars 99

Easy Garlic Escargots 100

Shoepeg Corn Salad 101

BBQ Teriyaki Pork Kabobs 101

Maria's Pepper Steak.. 102

Mama's Blackberry Cobbler 103

Hot Pepper Sauce - A Trinidadian Staple... 104

Raspberry Jalapeno Jelly.. 104

Chicken Kabobs

Prep: 15 mins **Cook:** 15 mins **Total:** 30 mins **Servings:** 4 **Yield:** 4 servings

Ingredients

- 4 breast half, bone and skin removed (blank)s skinless, boneless chicken breast halves - cubed
- 1 large green bell pepper, cut into 2 inch pieces
- 1 onion, cut into wedges
- 1 large red bell pepper, cut into 2 inch pieces
- 1 cup barbeque sauce
- 4 eaches skewers

Directions

Step 1

Preheat grill for high heat.

Step 2

Thread the chicken, green bell pepper, onion, and red bell pepper pieces onto skewers alternately.

Step 3

Lightly oil the grill grate. Place kabobs on the prepared grill, and brush with barbeque sauce. Cook, turning and brushing with barbeque sauce frequently, for 15 minutes, or until chicken juices run clear.

Nutrition Facts

Per Serving:

256 calories; protein 25.6g 51% DV; carbohydrates 29.6g 10% DV; fat 3.2g 5% DV; cholesterol 67.2mg 22% DV; sodium 761.8mg 31% DV.

Tony's Summer Pasta

Prep: 10 mins **Cook:** 5 mins **Total:** 15 mins **Servings:** 6 **Yield:** 6 servings

Ingredients

- 1 (16 ounce) package linguini pasta
- 6 plum tomato (blank)s roma (plum) tomatoes, chopped
- 1 pound shredded mozzarella cheese
- ⅓ cup chopped fresh basil
- 6 cloves garlic, minced
- ½ cup olive oil
- ½ teaspoon garlic salt
- ground black pepper to taste

Directions

Step 1

Combine tomatoes, cheese, basil, garlic, olive oil, garlic salt, and black pepper in medium bowl. Set aside.

Step 2

Meanwhile, cook pasta according to package directions.

Step 3

Drain pasta, and transfer to a serving bowl. Toss with tomato mixture. Serve.

Nutrition Facts

Per Serving:

635.3 calories; protein 29.1g 58% DV; carbohydrates 60g 19% DV; fat 31.9g 49% DV; cholesterol 48.4mg 16% DV; sodium 627.3mg 25% DV.

Blueberry Crumb Pie

Prep: 30 mins **Cook:** 40 mins **Total:** 1 hr 10 mins **Servings:** 8 **Yield:** 1 - 9 inch pie

Ingredients

- 1 (9 inch) unbaked pie crust
- ¾ cup white sugar
- ⅓ cup all-purpose flour
- 2 teaspoons grated lemon zest
- 1 tablespoon lemon juice
- 5 cups fresh or frozen blueberries
- ⅔ cup packed brown sugar
- ¾ cup rolled oats
- ½ cup all-purpose flour
- ½ teaspoon ground cinnamon
- 6 tablespoons butter

Directions

Step 1

Preheat the oven to 375 degrees F (190 degrees C).

Step 2

Press the pie crust into the bottom and up the sides of a 9 inch pie plate. In a large bowl, stir together the sugar and flour. Mix in the lemon zest and lemon juice. Gently stir in the blueberries. Pour into the pie crust.

Step 3

In a medium bowl, stir together the brown sugar, oats, flour and cinnamon. Mix in butter using a fork until crumbly. Spread the crumb topping evenly over the pie filling.

Step 4

Bake for 40 minutes in the preheated oven, or until browned on top. Cool over a wire rack.

Nutrition Facts

Per Serving:

461.2 calories; protein 4.5g 9% DV; carbohydrates 75.6g 24% DV; fat 17g 26% DV; cholesterol 22.9mg 8% DV; sodium 185mg 7% DV.

Triple Berry Crisp

Prep: 20 mins **Cook:** 40 mins **Total:** 1 hr **Servings:** 18 **Yield:** 18 servings

Ingredients

- 1 ½ cups fresh blackberries
- 1 ½ cups fresh raspberries
- 1 ½ cups fresh blueberries
- 4 tablespoons white sugar
- 2 cups all-purpose flour
- 2 cups rolled oats
- 1 ½ cups packed brown sugar
- 1 teaspoon ground cinnamon
- ½ teaspoon ground nutmeg
- 1 ½ cups butter

Directions

Step 1
Preheat oven to 350 degrees F (175 degrees C).

Step 2
In a large bowl, gently toss together blackberries, raspberries, blueberries, and white sugar; set aside.

Step 3
In a separate large bowl, combine flour, oats, brown sugar, cinnamon, and nutmeg. Cut in butter until crumbly. Press half of mixture in the bottom of a 9x13 inch pan. Cover with berries. Sprinkle remaining crumble mixture over the berries.

Step 4
Bake in the preheated oven for 30 to 40 minutes, or until fruit is bubbly and topping is golden brown.

Nutrition Facts
Per Serving:

294.8 calories; protein 3.2g 6% DV; carbohydrates 35.6g 12% DV; fat 16.3g 25% DV; cholesterol 40.7mg 14% DV; sodium 113.4mg 5% DV.

Crab and Shrimp Louis

Prep: 15 mins **Total:** 15 mins **Servings:** 4 **Yield:** 4 servings

Ingredients

- 4 large eggs eggs

- 1 head iceberg lettuce, shredded
- ¼ cucumber, thinly sliced
- ½ pound crabmeat
- 8 ounces cooked shrimp
- 1 avocado - peeled, pitted and sliced
- 8 eaches cherry tomatoes, halved
- ⅔ cup mayonnaise
- ⅓ cup hot chile sauce
- 2 tablespoons sweet pickle relish
- salt and pepper to taste
- 1 tablespoon chopped fresh parsley
- 1 lemon - cut into wedges, for garnish

Directions

Step 1

Place eggs in a saucepan and cover with cold water. Bring water to a boil; cover, remove from heat, and let eggs stand in hot water for 10 to 12 minutes. Remove from hot water, cool, peel and chop.

Step 2

Evenly divide the lettuce, cucumbers, crab, shrimp, avocado, tomatoes and eggs between 4 salad plates.

Step 3

Prepare the dressing by whisking together the mayonnaise, chili sauce, relish, salt and pepper. Spoon dressing over the salad and garnish with parsley and lemon.

Nutrition Facts

Per Serving:

581.4 calories; protein 34.3g 69% DV; carbohydrates 19g 6% DV; fat 43.2g 67% DV; cholesterol 352.3mg 117% DV; sodium 700.7mg 28% DV.

Cauliflower Salad

Prep: 25 mins **Cook:** 10 mins **Additional:** 2 hrs **Total:** 2 hrs 35 mins **Servings:** 6 **Yield:** 6 servings

Ingredients

- 1 head cauliflower, trimmed and cut into bite-size florets
- ¾ cup mayonnaise
- 1 tablespoon mustard
- 1 teaspoon salt
- 1 dash ground black pepper to taste
- 3 large eggs hard boiled eggs, chopped
- 1 onion, chopped
- ¾ cup frozen green peas, thawed

- ¼ cup dill pickles, chopped
- 3 slices crisply cooked bacon, crumbled

Directions

Step 1

Place cauliflower in a large saucepan and cover with water. Bring to a boil and cook until just fork tender, about 10 minutes. Drain and cool slightly.

Step 2

In a large bowl whisk together the mayonnaise, mustard, salt, and pepper. Add the cauliflower, eggs, onion, peas, dill pickles, and bacon to the dressing and stir until well coated. Cover and refrigerate for 2 to 24 hours. The longer the cauliflower salad chills, the better the flavor.

Nutrition Facts

Per Serving:

290.1 calories; protein 6.9g 14% DV; carbohydrates 12.8g 4% DV; fat 24.6g 38% DV; cholesterol 103.4mg 35% DV; sodium 742.2mg 30% DV.

Fettuccine with Sweet Pepper-Cayenne Sauce

Prep: 5 mins **Cook:** 10 mins **Total:** 15 mins **Servings:** 4 **Yield:** 4 servings

Ingredients

- 12 ounces dry fettuccine pasta
- 2 medium (blank)s red bell peppers, julienned
- 3 cloves garlic, minced
- ¾ teaspoon cayenne pepper
- 1 cup reduced fat sour cream
- ¾ cup chicken broth
- ¾ cup grated Parmesan cheese
- salt and pepper to taste

Directions

Step 1

Bring a large pot of lightly salted water to a boil. Add pasta and cook for 8 to 10 minutes or until al dente; drain.

Step 2

Meanwhile, spray cooking oil in a large skillet and saute red bell peppers, garlic and cayenne pepper over medium heat for 3 to 5 minutes.

Step 3

Stir in sour cream and broth; simmer uncovered for 5 minutes. Remove from heat and stir in cheese.

Step 4

Toss hot pasta with sauce and season with salt and pepper to taste; serve.

Tips

Please note that the magazine version of this recipe reduces the chicken broth amount an includes fresh basil as a garnish.

Nutrition Facts

Per Serving:

475 calories; protein 20.3g 41% DV; carbohydrates 69.3g 22% DV; fat 13.9g 21% DV; cholesterol 36.8mg 12% DV; sodium 403.2mg 16% DV.

Tomato Basil Salmon

Prep: 10 mins **Cook:** 20 mins **Total:** 30 mins **Servings:** 2 **Yield:** 2 salmon fillets

Ingredients

- 2 (6 ounce) boneless salmon fillets
- 1 tablespoon dried basil
- 1 tomato, thinly sliced
- 1 tablespoon olive oil
- 2 tablespoons grated Parmesan cheese

Directions

Step 1

Preheat oven to 375 degrees F (190 degrees C). Line a baking sheet with a piece of aluminum foil, and spray with nonstick cooking spray. Place the salmon fillets onto the foil, sprinkle with basil, top with tomato slices, drizzle with olive oil, and sprinkle with the Parmesan cheese.

Step 2

Bake in the preheated oven until the salmon is opaque in the center, and the Parmesan cheese is lightly browned on top, about 20 minutes.

Nutrition Facts

Per Serving:

405.4 calories; protein 36.2g 72% DV; carbohydrates 4g 1% DV; fat 26.6g 41% DV; cholesterol 103.5mg 35% DV; sodium 179.5mg 7% DV.

Easy Peach Cobbler with Cake Mix

Servings: 12 **Yield:** 12 servings

Ingredients

- 12 medium (2-1/2" dia) (approx 4 per lb)s fresh peaches, pitted and sliced
- 1 cup water
- 1 cup white sugar
- ½ teaspoon ground cinnamon

- 1 (18.25 ounce) package white cake mix
- 1 (8 ounce) package cream cheese
- ½ cup butter

Directions

Step 1

Preheat oven to 350 degrees F (175 degrees C).

Step 2

Spread peach slices evenly into a 9x13 inch baking dish. If using canned peach juice, pour 1 cup of it over peach slices. If using fresh peaches, combine water and sugar in a small bowl. Stir to dissolve, then pour mixture over peaches.

Step 3

Sprinkle cinnamon over peach slices, followed by dry cake mix. Top cake mix with pats of cream cheese. Dot cobbler with butter or margarine.

Step 4

Bake in preheated oven for 45 minutes, until golden.

Nutrition Facts

Per Serving:

403.8 calories; protein 3.4g 7% DV; carbohydrates 56.4g 18% DV; fat 18.8g 29% DV; cholesterol 40.9mg 14% DV; sodium 397mg 16% DV.

Good for You Greek Salad

Prep: 15 mins **Total:** 15 mins **Servings:** 6 **Yield:** 6 servings

Ingredients

- 3 large ripe tomatoes, chopped
- 2 medium (blank)s cucumbers, peeled and chopped
- 1 small red onion, chopped
- ¼ cup olive oil
- 4 teaspoons lemon juice
- 1 ½ teaspoons dried oregano
- salt and pepper to taste
- 1 cup crumbled feta cheese
- 6 eaches black Greek olives, pitted and sliced

Directions

Step 1

In shallow salad bowl, or on serving platter, combine tomatoes, cucumber, and onion. Sprinkle with oil, lemon juice, oregano, and salt and pepper to taste. Sprinkle feta cheese and olives over salad. Serve.

Nutrition Facts

Per Serving:

187.2 calories; protein 5g 10% DV; carbohydrates 8.3g 3% DV; fat 15.6g 24% DV; cholesterol 22.3mg 7% DV; sodium 346.8mg 14% DV.

Refreshing Cucumber Lemonade

Prep: 15 mins **Cook:** 5 mins **Additional:** 30 mins **Total:** 50 mins **Servings:** 4 **Yield:** 2 1/2 cups

Ingredients

- 1 cup water
- ½ cup white sugar
- 1 cucumber, sliced
- 6 eaches lemons, juiced

Directions

Step 1

Make a simple syrup by stirring the water and sugar together in a saucepan over medium heat; heat until just about to boil and the sugar has dissolved. Place in refrigerator 30 minutes, or until cool.

Step 2

Place the cucumber slices in a blender or food processor; blend until mashed into a pulp. Pour the cucumber pulp into a fine mesh strainer place over a bowl to catch the liquid; allow to sit until you have about 2/3 cup of liquid from the cucumber, about 15 minutes.

Step 3

Stir the simple syrup, cucumber liquid, and lemon juice together in a pitcher. Serve cold.

Nutrition Facts

Per Serving:

140.9 calories; protein 2.5g 5% DV; carbohydrates 45.5g 15% DV; fat 0.6g 1% DV; cholesterolmg; sodium 8.2mg.

Fried Soft-Shell Crab

Prep: 20 mins **Cook:** 15 mins **Total:** 35 mins **Servings:** 4 **Yield:** 4 servings

Ingredients

- 4 crabs soft-shell crabs
- 1 egg
- ½ cup milk
- 1 cup all-purpose flour
- 1 pinch salt and pepper to taste
- 4 cups oil for frying, or as needed

Directions

Step 1

Clean each crab. Lift one pointed side of top shell and remove the gills by pulling them out. Put top shell back down and repeat on other side. On the bottom side remove tail flap by twisting and pulling off. Using a pair of scissors, remove the face by cutting behind the eyes. Rinse the crabs thoroughly with cold water. Dry on paper towels.

Step 2

Heat oil in a deep fryer to 365 degrees F (180 degrees F). In a shallow dish, whisk together the egg and milk using a fork. In a separate bowl, stir salt and pepper into the flour. Lightly salt the crab, then dip in the flour, dip in the egg, then in the flour again.

Step 3

Carefully place crabs into the deep-fryer. Cook for 1 to 2 minutes, or until golden brown on one side. Carefully turn over, and cook until golden on the other side. Drain on paper towels. Serve as soon as they are cool enough to eat. You can eat the whole crab.

Nutrition Facts

Per Serving:

357.9 calories; protein 9.1g 18% DV; carbohydrates 25.4g 8% DV; fat 24.4g 38% DV; cholesterol 65.2mg 22% DV; sodium 76mg 3% DV.

Chocolate Zucchini Muffins

Servings: 24 Yield: 2 dozen

Ingredients

- 3 large eggs eggs
- 2 cups white sugar
- 1 cup vegetable oil
- ⅓ cup unsweetened cocoa powder
- 1 ½ teaspoons vanilla extract
- 2 cups grated zucchini
- 3 cups all-purpose flour
- 1 teaspoon baking soda
- ½ teaspoon baking powder
- 1 teaspoon salt
- ¼ teaspoon ground cinnamon
- ¼ teaspoon ground nutmeg
- ¼ teaspoon ground cloves
- ¼ teaspoon ground cardamom

Directions

Step 1

Preheat oven to 350 degrees F (175 degrees C). Lightly grease or line two 12 cup muffin tins with paper liners.

Step 2

In a large bowl beat the eggs. Beat in the sugar and oil. Add the cocoa, vanilla, zucchini and stir well.

Step 3

Stir in the flour, baking soda, baking powder, salt, cinnamon, nutmeg, cloves and cardamom. Mix until just moist.

Step 4

Pour batter into prepared muffin tins filling 2/3 of the way full. Bake at 350 degrees F (175 degrees C) for 20 to 25 minutes. Remove from pan and let cool on a wire rack. Store loosely covered.

Nutrition Facts

Per Serving:

216.7 calories; protein 2.7g 6% DV; carbohydrates 29.7g 10% DV; fat 10.1g 16% DV; cholesterol 23.3mg 8% DV; sodium 169.8mg 7% DV.

Summer Corn Salad

Prep: 25 mins **Cook:** 20 mins **Total:** 45 mins **Servings:** 4 **Yield:** 4 servings

Ingredients

- 6 ears corn, husked and cleaned
- 3 large tomatoes, diced
- 1 large onion, diced
- ¼ cup chopped fresh basil
- ¼ cup olive oil
- 2 tablespoons white vinegar
- salt and pepper to taste

Directions

Step 1

Bring a large pot of lightly salted water to a boil. Cook corn in boiling water for 7 to 10 minutes, or until desired tenderness. Drain, cool, and cut kernels off the cob with a sharp knife.

Step 2

In a large bowl, toss together the corn, tomatoes, onion, basil, oil, vinegar, salt and pepper. Chill until serving.

Nutrition Facts

Per Serving:

305.5 calories; protein 6.2g 12% DV; carbohydrates 42.8g 14% DV; fat 15.6g 24% DV; cholesterolmg; sodium 8.7mg.

Chicken Salad with Bacon, Lettuce, and Tomato

Prep: 15 mins **Cook:** 15 mins **Additional:** 30 mins **Total:** 1 hr **Servings:** 6 **Yield:** 6 servings

Ingredients

- 5 slices bacon
- 3 cups diced cooked chicken
- 1 cup chopped fresh tomato
- 2 stalks celery, thinly sliced
- ¾ cup mayonnaise
- 2 tablespoons minced green onion
- 1 tablespoon chopped parsley
- 1 teaspoon lemon juice
- 1 dash Worcestershire sauce
- 1 pinch salt and ground black pepper to taste
- 12 leaves romaine lettuce
- 1 large avocado, sliced

Directions

Step 1

Place bacon in a large skillet and cook over medium-high heat, turning occasionally, until evenly browned, about 10 minutes. Drain bacon slices on paper towels; crumble.

Step 2

Stir chicken, bacon, tomato, and celery together in a bowl.

Step 3

Whisk mayonnaise, parsley, green onions, lemon juice, Worcestershire sauce, salt, and black pepper together in a bowl until dressing is smooth. Pour dressing over chicken mixture; toss to coat. Refrigerate until chilled, at least 30 minutes.

Step 4

Stir chicken mixture and serve over romaine lettuce leaves; garnish with avocado slices.

Nutrition Facts

Per Serving:

455.5 calories; protein 23.9g 48% DV; carbohydrates 7.5g 2% DV; fat 37.3g 57% DV; cholesterol 71.4mg 24% DV; sodium 395mg 16% DV.

Mediterranean Summer Tomatoes

Prep: 10 mins **Additional:** 5 mins **Total:** 15 mins **Servings:** 6 **Yield:** 6 Servings

Ingredients

- 5 medium whole (2-3/5" dia) (blank)s fresh tomatoes
- 5 eaches shallots, coarsely chopped
- ½ cup olive oil
- ¼ cup balsamic vinegar
- 1 loaf French bread, for dipping

Directions

Step 1

Core and slice the tomatoes, and arrange them in a serving dish. Sprinkle the shallots over the tomatoes. Whisk the olive oil and balsamic vinegar together with a fork, then pour over the tomatoes. Let stand for 5 minutes before serving, or refrigerate, covered, for up to 3 days. Eat with French bread, and dip the bread in the marinade when finished with the tomatoes.

Nutrition Facts

Per Serving:

432.7 calories; protein 10.9g 22% DV; carbohydrates 55.3g 18% DV; fat 19.7g 30% DV; cholesterolmg; sodium 504.9mg 20% DV.

Strawberry-Melon Summer Salad

Prep: 20 mins **Total:** 20 mins **Servings:** 6 **Yield:** 6 servings

Ingredients

- 1 cup lemon yogurt
- 1 tablespoon honey
- 1 teaspoon lemon juice
- 2 cups watermelon balls
- 2 cups cantaloupe balls
- 2 cups halved fresh strawberries

Directions

Step 1

In a salad bowl, whisk together the lemon yogurt, honey, and lemon juice until smooth, and gently fold in the watermelon balls, cantaloupe balls, and strawberries. Toss to coat, and serve.

Nutrition Facts

Per Serving:

99.7 calories; protein 3.3g 7% DV; carbohydrates 22.7g 7% DV; fat 0.4g 1% DV; cholesterol 0.7mg; sodium 38.6mg 2% DV.

Mid-Summer Italian Bread Salad

Prep: 10 mins **Total:** 10 mins **Servings:** 4 **Yield:** 4 to 6 servings

Ingredients

- 1 clove garlic
- 1 (1 pound) loaf Italian bread
- 1 cup chopped tomatoes
- 1 cup cucumber - peeled, seeded and chopped
- 1 cup chopped red onion
- 1 clove garlic, minced
- 2 cups chopped fresh basil
- ⅛ cup chopped fresh thyme
- ¼ cup olive oil
- 2 tablespoons balsamic vinegar

Directions

Step 1

Rub a peeled clove of garlic around a wooden salad bowl.

Step 2

Pull apart or chop the bread into bite-size pieces.

Step 3

In the prepared salad bowl, combine the bread, tomatoes, cucumbers, red onions, garlic, basil and thyme. Add enough olive oil and vinegar to lightly coat, toss and serve.

Nutrition Facts

Per Serving:

468.2 calories; protein 11.9g 24% DV; carbohydrates 65.6g 21% DV; fat 17.8g 27% DV; cholesterolmg; sodium 670.7mg 27% DV.

Tasty BBQ Corn on the Cob

Prep: 15 mins **Cook:** 30 mins **Total:** 45 mins **Servings:** 6 **Yield:** 6 servings

Ingredients

- 1 teaspoon chili powder
- ⅛ teaspoon dried oregano
- 1 pinch onion powder
- 1 pinch cayenne pepper to taste
- 1 pinch garlic powder to taste
- 1 pinch salt and pepper to taste
- ½ cup butter, softened
- 6 ears corn, husked and cleaned

Directions

Step 1

Preheat grill for medium-high heat.

Step 2

In a medium bowl, mix together the chili powder, oregano, onion powder, cayenne pepper, garlic powder, salt, and pepper. Blend in the softened butter. Apply this mixture to each ear of corn, and place each ear onto a piece of aluminum foil big enough to wrap the corn. Wrap like a burrito, and twist the ends to close.

Step 3

Place wrapped corn on the preheated grill, and cook 20 to 30 minutes, until tender when poked with a fork. Turn corn occasionally during cooking.

Nutrition Facts

Per Serving:

215.8 calories; protein 3.2g 6% DV; carbohydrates 17.7g 6% DV; fat 16.5g 25% DV; cholesterol 40.7mg 14% DV; sodium 127.1mg 5% DV.

Best Lemonade Ever

Prep: 30 mins **Cook:** 5 mins **Additional:** 4 hrs **Total:** 4 hrs 35 mins **Servings:** 10 **Yield:** 10 (8 ounce) servings

Ingredients

- 1 ¾ cups white sugar
- 8 cups water
- 1 ½ cups lemon juice

Directions

Step 1

In a small saucepan, combine sugar and 1 cup water. Bring to boil and stir to dissolve sugar. Allow to cool to room temperature, then cover and refrigerate until chilled.

Step 2

Remove seeds from lemon juice, but leave pulp. In pitcher, stir together chilled syrup, lemon juice and remaining 7 cups water.

Nutrition Facts

Per Serving:

144.6 calories; protein 0.1g; carbohydrates 38.2g 12% DV; fatg; cholesterolmg; sodium 6.1mg.

Grilled Pork Chops with Fresh Nectarine Salsa

Prep: 25 mins **Cook:** 8 mins **Total:** 33 mins **Servings:** 4 **Yield:** 4 servings

Ingredients

- 2 eaches nectarines, pitted and diced
- 1 ripe tomato, seeded and diced

- ¼ cup diced onion
- 2 tablespoons chopped fresh cilantro
- 2 tablespoons fresh lime juice
- ¼ teaspoon crushed red pepper flakes, or to taste
- 1 pinch salt to taste
- 1 teaspoon ground cumin
- 1 teaspoon chili powder
- 1 pinch salt and ground black pepper to taste
- 2 tablespoons olive oil
- 8 (4 ounce) boneless pork loin chops

Directions

Step 1

Preheat an outdoor grill for medium-high heat. Lightly oil grate, and set 4 inches from the heat.

Step 2

To make the salsa, place the nectarines, tomato, onion, cilantro, lime juice, and red pepper flakes in a bowl; toss to blend. Season to taste with salt. Cover, and refrigerate 30 minutes to blend flavors.

Step 3

Stir the cumin, chili powder, salt, and pepper together in a small bowl. Place the olive oil in a small bowl. Brush the pork chops with oil, and season both sides evenly with the cumin mixture.

Step 4

Place pork loin chops on the preheated grill. Cook until lightly browned and juices run clear, about 4 minutes on each side. Place pork chops on serving plates, and top with a generous spoonful of salsa.

Nutrition Facts

Per Serving:

419 calories; protein 51.2g 103% DV; carbohydrates 10.8g 4% DV; fat 18.3g 28% DV; cholesterol 130.2mg 43% DV; sodium 91.9mg 4% DV.

Insalata Caprese II

Prep: 15 mins **Total:** 15 mins **Servings:** 6 **Yield:** 6 servings

Ingredients

- 4 large ripe tomatoes, sliced 1/4 inch thick
- 1 pound fresh mozzarella cheese, sliced 1/4 inch thick
- ⅓ cup fresh basil leaves
- 3 tablespoons extra virgin olive oil
- ½ teaspoon fine sea salt to taste
- 1 pinch freshly ground black pepper to taste

Directions

Step 1

On a large platter, alternate and overlap the tomato slices, mozzarella cheese slices, and basil leaves. Drizzle with olive oil. Season with sea salt and pepper.

Nutrition Facts

Per Serving:

310.6 calories; protein 17.9g 36% DV; carbohydrates 6.6g 2% DV; fat 23.9g 37% DV; cholesterol 59.8mg 20% DV; sodium 627.3mg 25% DV.

Fresh Peach Cobbler I

Prep: 30 mins **Cook:** 25 mins **Total:** 55 mins **Servings:** 6 **Yield:** 6 servings

Ingredients

Peach Filling:

- ½ cup white sugar
- 1 tablespoon cornstarch
- ¼ teaspoon ground cinnamon
- 4 cups sliced fresh peaches
- 1 teaspoon lemon juice

Cobbler Topping:

- 1 cup all-purpose flour
- 1 tablespoon white sugar
- 1 ½ teaspoons baking powder
- ½ teaspoon salt
- 3 tablespoons shortening
- ½ cup milk

Directions

Step 1

Preheat oven to 400 degrees F (200 degrees C).

Step 2

Combine 1/2 cup sugar, cornstarch, and cinnamon in a saucepan and whisk to mix. Stir in sliced peaches (see Editor's Note) and lemon juice, tossing until peaches are evenly coated.

Step 3

Cook filling over medium heat, stirring constantly, until mixture thickens and boils. Boil 1 minute. Pour mixture into an ungreased 2-quart casserole dish. Keep mixture hot in oven while you make the topping.

Step 4

In a medium bowl combine flour, 1 tablespoon sugar, baking powder, and salt. Mix thoroughly, then cut in shortening until mixture looks like fine crumbs. Add milk and stir until mixture is evenly moistened.

Step 5

Remove peach filling from oven and drop dough onto peaches in 6 equal-size spoonfuls.

Step 6

Return cobbler to oven and bake until topping is golden brown, 25 to 30 minutes.

Nutrition Facts

Per Serving:

242.8 calories; protein 2.9g 6% DV; carbohydrates 42.5g 14% DV; fat 7g 11% DV; cholesterol 1.6mg 1% DV; sodium 328mg 13% DV.

Amelia's Tuna Macaroni Salad

Prep: 20 mins **Total:** 20 mins **Servings:** 6 **Yield:** 6 servings

Ingredients

- 1 (12 ounce) package elbow macaroni
- 1 (5 ounce) can tuna, drained
- 2 stalks celery, chopped
- 2 tablespoons chopped sweet onion
- 1 (10 ounce) can baby peas, drained
- 1 cup mayonnaise
- 2 tablespoons sweet pickle relish
- 1 pinch salt and pepper to taste
- 3 large eggs hard-cooked eggs, quartered
- 1 pinch paprika, for garnish

Directions

Step 1

Bring a large pot of lightly salted water to a boil. Add the macaroni, and cook until tender, about 8 minutes. Drain and rinse under cold running water.

Step 2

In a large bowl, stir together the macaroni, tuna, celery, onion and peas. Mix in the mayonnaise, relish, salt and pepper. Garnish with egg wedges and a sprinkle of paprika. Cover and chill for at least 1 hour before serving.

Nutrition Facts

Per Serving:

582 calories; protein 18.7g 37% DV; carbohydrates 51.6g 17% DV; fat 33.4g 51% DV; cholesterol 126.2mg 42% DV; sodium 416mg 17% DV.

Mom's Zucchini Bread

Prep: 20 mins **Cook:** 1 hr **Additional:** 20 mins **Total:** 1 hr 40 mins **Servings:** 24 **Yield:** 2 loaves

Ingredients

- 3 cups all-purpose flour
- 1 teaspoon salt
- 1 teaspoon baking soda
- 1 teaspoon baking powder
- 1 tablespoon ground cinnamon
- 3 large eggs eggs
- 1 cup vegetable oil
- 2 ¼ cups white sugar
- 3 teaspoons vanilla extract
- 2 cups grated zucchini
- 1 cup chopped walnuts

Directions

Step 1

Grease and flour two 8 x 4 inch pans. Preheat oven to 325 degrees F (165 degrees C).

Step 2

Sift flour, salt, baking powder, soda, and cinnamon together in a bowl.

Step 3

Beat eggs, oil, vanilla, and sugar together in a large bowl. Add sifted ingredients to the creamed mixture, and beat well. Stir in zucchini and nuts until well combined. Pour batter into prepared pans.

Step 4

Bake for 40 to 60 minutes, or until tester inserted in the center comes out clean. Cool in pan on rack for 20 minutes. Remove bread from pan, and completely cool.

Nutrition Facts

Per Serving:

255.2 calories; protein 3.3g 7% DV; carbohydrates 32.1g 10% DV; fat 13.1g 20% DV; cholesterol 23.3mg 8% DV; sodium 179.8mg 7% DV.

Grilled Steak Salad with Asian Dressing

Prep: 30 mins **Cook:** 15 mins **Additional:** 1 hr **Total:** 1 hr 45 mins **Servings:** 2 **Yield:** 2 servings

Ingredients

- 1 (12 ounce) rib eye steak
- 1 tablespoon soy sauce
- 1 teaspoon Montreal steak seasoning, or to taste
- ½ lemon, juiced
- 2 tablespoons rice vinegar
- 2 tablespoons olive oil

- 2 tablespoons white sugar
- ½ teaspoon sesame oil
- ¼ teaspoon garlic powder
- 2 pinches red pepper flakes
- 10 leaves romaine lettuce, torn into bite-size pieces
- ½ large English cucumber, cubed
- 1 avocado - peeled, pitted, and diced
- 1 tomato, cut into wedges
- 1 carrot, grated
- 4 thin slices red onion
- 3 tablespoons toasted sesame seeds

Directions

Step 1

Season both side of the rib eye steak with soy sauce and steak seasoning. Cover and refrigerate at least 1 hour to overnight.

Step 2

Preheat an outdoor grill for medium-high heat and lightly oil the grate.

Step 3

Grill steak on preheated grill until firm, reddish-pink, and juicy in the center, about 6 minutes per side. An instant-read thermometer inserted into the center should read 130 degrees F (54 degrees C). Transfer steak to a platter, sprinkle with lemon juice, and cover loosely with aluminum foil. Allow meat to rest for about 10 minutes, then cut into strips.

Step 4

Whisk rice vinegar, olive oil, sugar, sesame oil, garlic powder, and red pepper flakes together in a small bowl. Combine lettuce, cucumber, avocado, tomato, carrot, red onion, and steak strips in a large bowl. Pour rice vinegar dressing over salad and toss to coat. Sprinkle with sesame seeds to serve.

Nutrition Facts

Per Serving:

704.3 calories; protein 26g 52% DV; carbohydrates 38.9g 13% DV; fat 52.6g 81% DV; cholesterol 60.7mg 20% DV; sodium 1000.5mg 40% DV.

Fresh Peach Trifle

Prep: 35 mins **Total:** 35 mins **Servings:** 8 **Yield:** 8 servings

Ingredients

- 6 large ripe peaches - peeled, pitted and sliced
- 1 tablespoon fresh lemon juice
- 2 (8 ounce) containers vanilla yogurt

- 1 teaspoon lemon zest
- 1 (10 inch) prepared angel food cake

Directions

Step 1

Place peaches in a large bowl, and gently toss with lemon juice. Place 1 cup of peaches in a blender, set aside remaining slices, and blend until smooth. Place yogurt into a bowl; stir in the peach puree and lemon zest until well blended.

Step 2

Cut the angel food cake into squares and place half in the bottom of a glass dish. Spoon half of the peach slices over the cake. Cover with half of the yogurt mixture. Place remaining cake squares over the yogurt. Top with peaches, reserving 5 or 6 slices for garnish. Cover with remaining yogurt mixture. Garnish with peach slices. Refrigerate until ready to serve.

Nutrition Facts

Per Serving:

182.1 calories; protein 5.3g 11% DV; carbohydrates 38.3g 12% DV; fat 1g 2% DV; cholesterol 2.8mg 1% DV; sodium 356mg 14% DV.

Jersey Fresh Tomato Soup

Prep: 30 mins **Cook:** 1 hr 30 mins **Total:** 2 hrs **Servings:** 4 **Yield:** 4 servings

Ingredients

- 7 cups peeled, seeded, and chopped tomatoes
- 1 cup finely chopped carrots
- ¾ cup finely chopped onion
- 1 (13.75 ounce) can chicken broth
- 1 tablespoon white sugar
- 2 teaspoons sea salt
- 3 tablespoons butter
- 3 tablespoons all-purpose flour
- 1 cup 2% milk
- 2 teaspoons dried basil
- ½ teaspoon celery salt
- ½ teaspoon ground black pepper
- ¼ teaspoon garlic powder

Directions

Step 1

Bring the tomatoes, carrots, and onion to a boil over medium-high heat in a stockpot, then reduce heat to medium-low. Simmer for 30 minutes. Stir in the chicken broth, sugar, and salt.

Step 2

Melt the butter over medium-low heat in a small saucepan. Whisk in the flour, stirring until thick. Slowly whisk in the milk until smooth. Cook and stir, whisking constantly until thickened, about 5 minutes, then stir milk mixture in to the stockpot. Season with basil, celery salt, black pepper, and garlic powder. Continue to simmer the soup on low to reduce and thicken, about 1 hour.

Cook's Note:

A food processor can be used to finely chop the carrots and onion. An immersion blender can be used for a smooth texture.

Nutrition Facts

Per Serving:

233.6 calories; protein 6.8g 14% DV; carbohydrates 30g 10% DV; fat 10.9g 17% DV; cholesterol 30.2mg 10% DV; sodium 1665.7mg 67% DV.

Watermelon and Feta Salad with Arugula and Spinach

Prep: 20 mins **Total:** 20 mins **Servings:** 4 **Yield:** 8 cups

Ingredients

- 3 tablespoons extra-virgin olive oil
- 2 teaspoons white balsamic vinegar
- ½ teaspoon kosher salt
- 2 cups arugula
- 2 cups baby spinach leaves
- 1 cup thinly sliced red onion
- 1 cup grape tomatoes, halved
- ½ cup crumbled feta cheese
- 2 cups bite sized watermelon chunks

Directions

Step 1

Whisk the olive oil, white balsamic vinegar, and salt together in a small bowl; set aside.

Step 2

Combine the arugula, spinach, onions, and tomatoes in a large salad bowl. Drizzle the vinaigrette over the salad mixture; toss to coat. Add the feta cheese and watermelon to serve.

Nutrition Facts

Per Serving:

190.8 calories; protein 4.5g 9% DV; carbohydrates 12.3g 4% DV; fat 14.5g 22% DV; cholesterol 16.7mg 6% DV; sodium 469.8mg 19% DV.

Slow Cooker Lemon Garlic Chicken II

Prep: 15 mins **Cook:** 3 hrs 15 mins **Total:** 3 hrs 30 mins **Servings:** 6 **Yield:** 6 servings

Ingredients

- 1 teaspoon dried oregano
- ½ teaspoon salt
- ¼ teaspoon ground black pepper
- 2 pounds skinless, boneless chicken breast halves
- 2 tablespoons butter
- ¼ cup water
- 3 tablespoons fresh lemon juice
- 2 cloves garlic, minced
- 1 teaspoon chicken bouillon granules
- 1 teaspoon chopped fresh parsley

Directions

Step 1

In a bowl, mix the oregano, salt, and pepper. Rub the mixture into chicken. Melt the butter in a skillet over medium heat. Brown chicken in butter for 3 to 5 minutes on each side. Place chicken in a slow cooker.

Step 2

In the same skillet, mix the water, lemon juice, garlic, and bouillon. Bring the mixture to boil. Pour over the chicken in the slow cooker.

Step 3

Cover, and cook on High for 3 hours, or Low for 6 hours. Add the parsley to the slow cooker 15 to 30 minutes before the end of the cook time.

Nutrition Facts
Per Serving:
192.3 calories; protein 29.6g 59% DV; carbohydrates 1.3g; fat 7g 11% DV; cholesterol 88.2mg 29% DV; sodium 347.6mg 14% DV.

Strawberry Shortcake

Prep: 30 mins **Cook:** 20 mins **Total:** 50 mins **Servings:** 8 **Yield:** 1 8-inch round cake

Ingredients

- 3 pints fresh strawberries
- ½ cup white sugar
- 2 ¼ cups all-purpose flour
- 4 teaspoons baking powder
- 2 tablespoons white sugar

- ¼ teaspoon salt
- ⅓ cup shortening
- 1 egg
- ⅔ cup milk
- 2 cups whipped heavy cream

Directions

Step 1

Slice the strawberries and toss them with 1/2 cup of white sugar. Set aside.

Step 2

Preheat oven to 425 degrees F (220 degrees C). Grease and flour one 8 inch round cake pan.

Step 3

In a medium bowl combine the flour, baking powder, 2 tablespoons white sugar and the salt. With a pastry blender cut in the shortening until the mixture resembles coarse crumbs. Make a well in the center and add the beaten egg and milk. Stir until just combined.

Step 4

Spread the batter into the prepared pan. Bake at 425 degrees F (220 degrees C) for 15 to 20 minutes or until golden brown. Let cool partially in pan on wire rack.

Step 5

Slice partially cooled cake in half, making two layers. Place half of the strawberries on one layer and top with the other layer. Top with remaining strawberries and cover with the whipped cream.

Nutrition Facts

Per Serving:

430.2 calories; protein 6.6g 13% DV; carbohydrates 55.2g 18% DV; fat 21.4g 33% DV; cholesterol 65.8mg 22% DV; sodium 347mg 14% DV.

Fresh Tomato Basil Sauce

Prep: 20 mins **Cook:** 2 hrs **Total:** 2 hrs 20 mins **Servings:** 6 **Yield:** 6 servings

Ingredients

- 8 pounds tomatoes, seeded and diced
- ¼ cup chopped fresh basil
- 1 large onion, minced
- 3 cloves garlic, minced
- ½ cup olive oil
- salt and pepper to taste

Directions

Step 1

In large saucepan, cook tomatoes and basil over medium-low heat until tomatoes are soft.

Step 2

Meanwhile, in medium skillet, saute onion and garlic in olive oil until onions are translucent.

Step 3

Add onion mixture to tomato mixture and add salt and pepper. Let simmer on low heat for 2 hours or until thick.

Nutrition Facts

Per Serving:

330.2 calories; protein 6.9g 14% DV; carbohydrates 37.8g 12% DV; fat 20.6g 32% DV; cholestcrolmg; sodium 69.5mg 3% DV.

Creamy Garlic Sauce

Prep: 2 mins **Cook:** 5 mins **Total:** 7 mins **Servings:** 4 **Yield:** 4 servings

Ingredients

- ½ cup water, divided
- 2 tablespoons chopped garlic
- 1 teaspoon garlic powder
- 2 cups heavy cream
- 1 tablespoon chopped fresh parsley
- 1 pinch salt and pepper to taste
- 2 tablespoons cornstarch

Directions

Step 1

Pour half of the water into a saucepan, and bring to a boil over medium heat. Add the garlic and garlic powder, and boil until the water has almost evaporated, about 5 minutes. Stir in the heavy cream, parsley, salt, and pepper. Mix the cornstarch with the remaining water, and stir into the sauce. Cook, stirring constantly, until thickened, about 3 minutes.

Nutrition Facts

Per Serving:

434.7 calories; protein 2.9g 6% DV; carbohydrates 8.9g 3% DV; fat 44.1g 68% DV; cholesterol 163mg 54% DV; sodium 47mg 2% DV.

Juicy Peach Crisp

Prep: 15 mins **Cook:** 45 mins **Total:** 1 hr **Servings:** 6 **Yield:** 6 servings

Ingredients

- 6 medium (2-1/2" dia) (approx 4 per lb)s fresh peaches - peeled, pitted, and sliced
- ½ teaspoon almond extract

- 1 cup all-purpose flour
- 1 cup white sugar
- ¼ cup brown sugar
- ½ teaspoon ground cinnamon
- ¼ teaspoon salt
- ½ cup butter

Directions

Step 1

Preheat an oven to 375 degrees F (190 degrees C), and grease an 8 inch square baking dish.

Step 2

Place the peaches in the bottom of the baking dish, and sprinkle them with almond extract.

Step 3

In a bowl, combine the flour, sugar, brown sugar, cinnamon, and salt. Cut the butter into the flour mixture with a pastry cutter until the mixture resembles crumbs.

Step 4

Sprinkle the flour mixture in an even layer over the top of the peaches, and bake in the preheated oven for about 45 minutes, until the peaches are bubbling and the topping is browned.

Nutrition Facts

Per Serving:

401.5 calories; protein 2.4g 5% DV; carbohydrates 64.4g 21% DV; fat 15.6g 24% DV; cholesterol 40.7mg 14% DV; sodium 212.8mg 9% DV.

Blueberry Cream Muffins

Prep: 10 mins **Cook:** 20 mins **Total:** 30 mins **Servings:** 24 **Yield:** 2 dozen

Ingredients

- 4 large eggs eggs
- 2 cups white sugar
- 1 cup vegetable oil
- 1 teaspoon vanilla extract
- 4 cups all-purpose flour
- 1 teaspoon salt
- 1 teaspoon baking soda
- 2 cups sour cream
- 2 cups blueberries

Directions

Step 1

Preheat oven to 400 degrees F (200 degrees C). Grease 24 muffin cups or line with paper muffin liners.

Step 2

In large bowl beat eggs, gradually add sugar while beating. Continue beating while slowly pouring in oil. Stir in vanilla. In a separate bowl, stir together flour, salt and baking soda.

Step 3

Stir dry ingredients into egg mixture alternately with sour cream. Gently fold in blueberries. Scoop batter into prepared muffin cups.

Step 4

Bake in preheated oven for 20 minutes.

Nutrition Facts

Per Serving:

281 calories; protein 3.9g 8% DV; carbohydrates 35.2g 11% DV; fat 14.2g 22% DV; cholesterol 39.4mg 13% DV; sodium 171.7mg 7% DV.

Rosemary Ranch Chicken Kabobs

Prep: 50 mins **Cook:** 10 mins **Total:** 1 hr **Servings:** 6 **Yield:** 6 servings

Ingredients

- ½ cup olive oil
- ½ cup ranch dressing
- 3 tablespoons Worcestershire sauce
- 1 tablespoon minced fresh rosemary
- 2 teaspoons salt
- 1 teaspoon lemon juice
- 1 teaspoon white vinegar
- ¼ teaspoon ground black pepper, or to taste
- 1 tablespoon white sugar, or to taste
- 5 eaches skinless, boneless chicken breast halves - cut into 1 inch cubes

Directions

Step 1

In a medium bowl, stir together the olive oil, ranch dressing, Worcestershire sauce, rosemary, salt, lemon juice, white vinegar, pepper, and sugar. Let stand for 5 minutes. Place chicken in the bowl, and stir to coat with the marinade. Cover and refrigerate for 30 minutes.

Step 2

Preheat the grill for medium-high heat. Thread chicken onto skewers and discard marinade.

Step 3

Lightly oil the grill grate. Grill skewers for 8 to 12 minutes, or until the chicken is no longer pink in the center, and the juices run clear.

Nutrition Facts

Per Serving:

377.7 calories; protein 19.9g 40% DV; carbohydrates 4.8g 2% DV; fat 30.7g 47% DV; cholesterol 59.2mg 20% DV; sodium 1097.2mg 44% DV.

Grilled Beef Tenderloin with Herb-Garlic-Pepper Coating

Prep: 30 mins **Cook:** 55 mins **Total:** 1 hr 25 mins **Servings:** 13 **Yield:** 13 (6-ounce) servings

Ingredients

- 1 (5 pound) whole beef tenderloin
- 6 tablespoons olive oil
- 8 large garlic cloves, minced
- 2 tablespoons minced fresh rosemary
- 1 tablespoon dried thyme leaves
- 2 tablespoons coarsely ground black pepper
- 1 tablespoon salt

Directions

Step 1

Prepare beef: Trim off excess fat with a sharp knife. Fold thin tip end under to approximate the thickness of the rest of the roast. Tie with butcher's twine, then keep tying the roast with twine every 11/2 to 2 inches (to help the roast keep its shape). Snip silverskin with scissors to keep roast from bowing during cooking. Then, mix oil, garlic, rosemary, thyme, pepper and salt; rub over roast to coat. Set meat aside.

Step 2

Either build a charcoal fire in half the grill or turn all gas burners on high for 10 minutes. Lubricate grate with an oil-soaked rag using tongs. Place beef on hot rack and close lid; grill until well-seared, about 5 minutes. Turn meat and close lid; grill until well-seared on second side, another 5 minutes.

Step 3

Move meat to the charcoal grill's cool side, or turn off burner directly underneath the meat and turn remaining one or two burners (depending on grill style) to medium. Cook until a meat thermometer inserted in the thickest section registers 130 degrees for rosy pink, 45 to 60 minutes, depending on tenderloin size and grill. Let meat rest 15 minutes before carving.

Nutrition Facts

Per Serving:

364.3 calories; protein 26.5g 53% DV; carbohydrates 1.9g 1% DV; fat 27.3g 42% DV; cholesterol 88.9mg 30% DV; sodium 599mg 24% DV.

Peach Muffins

Prep: 25 mins **Cook:** 25 mins **Total:** 50 mins **Servings:** 16 **Yield:** 16 muffins

Ingredients

- 3 cups all-purpose flour
- 1 tablespoon ground cinnamon
- 1 teaspoon baking soda
- 1 teaspoon salt
- 1 ¼ cups vegetable oil
- 3 large eggs eggs, lightly beaten
- 2 cups white sugar
- 2 cups peeled, pitted, and chopped peaches

Directions

Step 1

Preheat oven to 400 degrees F (200 degrees C). Grease the bottoms and sides of 16 muffin cups, or line with paper liners.

Step 2

In a large bowl, mix the flour, cinnamon, baking soda, and salt. In a separate bowl, mix the oil, eggs, and sugar. Stir the oil mixture into the flour mixture just until moist. Fold in the peaches. Spoon into the prepared muffin cups.

Step 3

Bake 25 minutes in the preheated oven, until a toothpick inserted in the center of a muffin comes out clean. Cool 10 minutes before turning out onto wire racks to cool completely.

Nutrition Facts

Per Serving:

351.1 calories; protein 3.6g 7% DV; carbohydrates 44.3g 14% DV; fat 18.2g 28% DV; cholesterol 34.9mg 12% DV; sodium 238.3mg 10% DV.

Mexican Corn on the Cob (Elote)

Prep: 10 mins **Cook:** 10 mins **Total:** 20 mins **Servings:** 4 **Yield:** 4 servings

Ingredients

- 4 ears corn, shucked
- ¼ cup melted butter
- ¼ cup mayonnaise
- ½ cup grated cotija cheese
- 4 wedges lime

Directions

Step 1

Preheat an outdoor grill for medium-high heat.

Step 2

Grill corn until hot and lightly charred all over, 7 to 10 minutes, depending on the temperature of the grill. Roll the ears in melted butter, then spread evenly with mayonnaise. Sprinkle with cotija cheese and serve with a lime wedge.

Nutrition Facts

Per Serving:

386.5 calories; protein 8.4g 17% DV; carbohydrates 28.9g 9% DV; fat 29.1g 45% DV; cholesterol 53.1mg 18% DV; sodium 368mg 15% DV.

Grilled Yellow Squash

Prep: 10 mins **Cook:** 20 mins **Total:** 30 mins **Servings:** 8 **Yield:** 8 servings

Ingredients

- 4 medium yellow squash
- ½ cup extra virgin olive oil
- 2 cloves garlic, crushed
- 1 pinch salt and pepper to taste

Directions

Step 1

Preheat the grill for medium heat.

Step 2

Cut the squash horizontally into 1/4 inch to 1/2 inch thick slices so that you have nice long strips that won't fall through the grill.

Step 3

Heat olive oil in a small pan, and add garlic cloves. Cook over medium heat until the garlic starts to sizzle and become fragrant. Brush the slices of squash with the garlic oil, and season with salt and pepper.

Step 4

Grill squash slices for 5 to 10 minutes per side, until they reach the desired tenderness. Brush with additional garlic oil, and turn occasionally to prevent sticking or burning.

Nutrition Facts

Per Serving:

145.7 calories; protein 1g 2% DV; carbohydrates 4.2g 1% DV; fat 14.2g 22% DV; cholesterolmg; sodium 2.1mg.

Caldo de Res (Mexican Beef Soup)

Prep: 30 mins **Cook:** 2 hrs **Total:** 2 hrs 30 mins **Servings:** 8 **Yield:** 8 servings

Ingredients

- 2 pounds beef shank, with bone

- 1 tablespoon vegetable oil
- 2 teaspoons salt
- 2 teaspoons ground black pepper
- 1 onion, chopped
- 1 (14.5 ounce) can diced tomatoes
- 3 cups beef broth
- 4 cups water
- 2 medium carrot, coarsely chopped
- ¼ cup chopped fresh cilantro
- 1 potato, quartered
- 2 ears corn, husked and cut into thirds
- 2 chayote, (5-3/4")s chayotes, quartered
- 1 medium head cabbage, cored and cut into wedges
- ¼ cup sliced pickled jalapenos
- ¼ cup finely chopped onion
- 1 cup chopped fresh cilantro
- 2 lime (2" dia)s limes, cut into wedges
- 4 medium (3/4" to 1" dia)s radishes, quartered

Directions

Step 1

Cut the meat from the beef bones into about 1/2 inch pieces, leaving some on the bones.

Step 2

Heat a heavy soup pot over medium-high heat until very hot. Add the oil, tilting the pan to coat the bottom. Add the meat and bones, and season with salt and pepper. Cook and stir until thoroughly browned.

Step 3

Add 1 onion, and cook until onion is also lightly browned. Stir in the tomatoes and broth. The liquid should cover the bones by 1/2 inch. If not, add enough water to compensate. Reduce heat to low, and simmer for 1 hour with the lid on loosely. If meat is not tender, continue cooking for another 10 minutes or so.

Step 4

Pour in the water, and return to a simmer. Add the carrot and 1/4 cup cilantro, and cook for 10 minutes, then stir in the potato, corn and chayote. Simmer until vegetables are tender. Push the cabbage wedges into the soup, and cook for about 10 more minutes.

Step 5

Ladle soup into large bowls, including meat vegetables and bones. Garnish with jalapenos, minced onion, and additional cilantro. Squeeze lime juice over all, and serve with radishes.

Nutrition Facts

Per Serving:

234.2 calories; protein 22g 44% DV; carbohydrates 25.9g 8% DV; fat 5.7g 9% DV; cholesterol 38.7mg 13% DV; sodium 1134.7mg 45% DV.

Tomato Basil Penne Pasta

Prep: 20 mins **Cook:** 25 mins **Total:** 45 mins **Servings:** 4 **Yield:** 4 servings

Ingredients

- 1 (8 ounce) package penne pasta
- 1 tablespoon basil oil
- 1 tablespoon olive oil
- 3 cloves garlic, minced
- 1 pint grape tomatoes, halved
- 1 cup shredded pepperjack cheese
- 1 cup shredded mozzarella cheese
- ¼ cup grated Parmesan cheese
- 1 tablespoon minced fresh basil

Directions

Step 1

Bring a large pot of water to a rolling boil over high heat. Cook pasta in boiling water until the pasta has cooked through, but is still firm to the bite, about 11 minutes. Drain.

Step 2

Heat basil and olive oils in a large skillet over medium-high heat. Cook garlic in oil until soft. Add tomatoes, reduce heat to medium, and simmer for 10 minutes. Stir in pepperjack, mozzarella, and Parmesan cheese. When cheese begins to melt, mix in cooked penne pasta. Season with fresh basil.

Cook's note:

Use 2 tablespoons olive oil if basil oil is unavailable.

Nutrition Facts

Per Serving:

502.4 calories; protein 24.1g 48% DV; carbohydrates 47.1g 15% DV; fat 24.8g 38% DV; cholesterol 57.8mg 19% DV; sodium 461.8mg 19% DV.

Greek Orzo Salad

Prep: 1 hr 10 mins **Cook:** 10 mins **Total:** 1 hr 20 mins **Servings:** 6 **Yield:** 6 servings

Ingredients

- 1 ½ cups uncooked orzo pasta
- 2 (6 ounce) cans marinated artichoke hearts
- 1 tomato, seeded and chopped

- 1 cucumber, seeded and chopped
- 1 red onion, chopped
- 1 cup crumbled feta cheese
- 1 (2 ounce) can black olives, drained
- ¼ cup chopped fresh parsley
- 1 tablespoon lemon juice
- ½ teaspoon dried oregano
- ½ teaspoon lemon pepper

Directions

Step 1

Bring a large pot of lightly salted water to a boil. Add pasta and cook for 8 to 10 minutes or until al dente; drain. Drain artichoke hearts, reserving liquid.

Step 2

In large bowl combine pasta, artichoke hearts, tomato, cucumber, onion, feta, olives, parsley, lemon juice, oregano and lemon pepper. Toss and chill for 1 hour in refrigerator.

Step 3

Just before serving, drizzle reserved artichoke marinade over salad.

Nutrition Facts

Per Serving:

325.8 calories; protein 13.1g 26% DV; carbohydrates 48.7g 16% DV; fat 10.2g 16% DV; cholesterol 22.3mg 7% DV; sodium 615.2mg 25% DV.

Cucumbers in Sour Cream

Prep: 10 mins **Additional:** 4 hrs **Total:** 4 hrs 10 mins **Servings:** 12 **Yield:** 3 cups

Ingredients

- 2 eaches cucumbers, thinly sliced
- 1 (8 ounce) container sour cream
- ¼ cup distilled white vinegar
- ⅓ cup white sugar
- 1 pinch salt and ground black pepper to taste

Directions

Step 1

Place the cucumber slices in a container and cover with cold water. Refrigerate 4 hours to overnight.

Step 2

Whisk the sour cream, vinegar, sugar, and salt in a mixing bowl until the sugar has dissolved. Drain the cucumbers and squeeze out the excess water; add to the bowl and mix to coat with dressing.

Nutrition Facts

Per Serving:

69.1 calories; protein 0.9g 2% DV; carbohydrates 8.1g 3% DV; fat 4g 6% DV; cholesterol 8.3mg 3% DV; sodium 11mg.

Key West Chicken

Prep: 15 mins **Cook:** 15 mins **Additional:** 30 mins **Total:** 1 hr **Servings:** 4 **Yield:** 4 servings

Ingredients

- 3 tablespoons soy sauce
- 1 tablespoon honey
- 1 tablespoon vegetable oil
- 1 teaspoon lime juice
- 1 teaspoon chopped garlic
- 4 breast half, bone and skin removed (blank)s skinless, boneless chicken breast halves

Directions

Step 1

In a shallow container, blend soy sauce, honey, vegetable oil, lime juice, and garlic. Place chicken breast halves into the mixture, and turn to coat. Cover, and marinate in the refrigerator at least 30 minutes.

Step 2

Preheat an outdoor grill for high heat.

Step 3

Lightly oil the grill grate. Discard marinade, and grill chicken 6 to 8 minutes on each side, until juices run clear.

Nutrition Facts

Per Serving:

184.1 calories; protein 25.3g 51% DV; carbohydrates 5.6g 2% DV; fat 6.2g 10% DV; cholesterol 67.2mg 22% DV; sodium 735.3mg 29% DV.

GA Peach Pound Cake

Prep: 20 mins **Cook:** 1 hr 10 mins **Total:** 1 hr 30 mins **Servings:** 16 **Yield:** 1 - 10 inch tube pan

Ingredients

- 1 cup butter or margarine, softened
- 2 cups white sugar
- 4 large eggs eggs
- 1 teaspoon vanilla extract
- 3 cups all-purpose flour
- 1 teaspoon baking powder

- ½ teaspoon salt
- 2 cups fresh peaches, pitted and chopped

Directions

Step 1

Preheat oven to 325 degrees F (165 degrees C). Butter a 10 inch tube pan and coat with white sugar.

Step 2

In a large bowl, cream together the butter and sugar until light and fluffy. Add the eggs one at a time, beating well with each addition, then stir in the vanilla. Reserve 1/4 cup of flour for later, and sift together the remaining flour, baking powder and salt. Gradually stir into the creamed mixture. Use the reserved flour to coat the chopped peaches, then fold the floured peaches into the batter. Spread evenly into the prepared pan.

Step 3

Bake for 60 to 70 minutes in the preheated oven, or until a toothpick inserted into the cake comes out clean. Allow cake to cool in the pan for 10 minutes, before inverting onto a wire rack to cool completely.

Nutrition Facts

Per Serving:

306.6 calories; protein 4.1g 8% DV; carbohydrates 44.1g 14% DV; fat 13g 20% DV; cholesterol 77mg 26% DV; sodium 195.7mg 8% DV.

Easy, Eggless Strawberry Ice Cream

Prep: 10 mins **Additional:** 50 mins **Total:** 1 hr **Servings:** 8 **Yield:** 8 servings

Ingredients

- 2 cups whole milk
- 2 cups heavy cream
- 1 cup white sugar
- ¼ teaspoon salt
- 2 teaspoons vanilla extract
- 2 cups mashed fresh strawberries
- 2 drops red food coloring

Directions

Step 1

In a large bowl, combine the milk, cream, sugar, salt, vanilla, strawberries, and food coloring. Pour the mixture into the freezer bowl of an ice cream maker, and freeze according to manufacturer's directions.

Nutrition Facts

Per Serving:

354.2 calories; protein 3.6g 7% DV; carbohydrates 34.1g 11% DV; fat 23.4g 36% DV; cholesterol 86.4mg 29% DV; sodium 121mg 5% DV.

Italian Stewed Tomatoes

Prep: 30 mins **Cook:** 10 mins **Total:** 40 mins **Servings:** 9 **Yield:** 7 pints

Ingredients

- 24 large tomatoes - peeled, seeded and chopped
- 1 cup chopped celery
- ½ cup chopped onion
- ¼ cup chopped green bell pepper
- 2 teaspoons dried basil
- 1 tablespoon white sugar

Directions

Step 1

In a large saucepan over medium heat, combine tomatoes, celery, onion, bell pepper, basil and sugar. Cover and cook for 10 minutes, stirring occasionally to prevent sticking.

Nutrition Facts

Per Serving:

100.5 calories; protein 4.6g 9% DV; carbohydrates 22.2g 7% DV; fat 1g 2% DV; cholesterolmg; sodium 34.4mg 1% DV.

Mom's Cucumbers

Servings: 5 **Yield:** 4 to 6 side salad servings

Ingredients

- 3 large cucumbers
- 1 teaspoon salt
- ¼ cup white sugar
- ⅛ cup water
- ¼ cup distilled white vinegar
- ½ teaspoon celery seed
- ¼ cup chopped onion

Directions

Step 1

Peel the cucumbers and slice wafer thin. Sprinkle with salt. Let stand 30 minutes, then squeeze cucumbers to release moisture.

Step 2

In a medium size bowl mix sugar, water, vinegar, celery seed, and onion. Add cucumbers to mixture. Mix well. Refrigerate 1 hour.

Nutrition Facts

Per Serving:

68.3 calories; protein 1.2g 2% DV; carbohydrates 17g 6% DV; fat 0.2g; cholesterolmg; sodium 469.1mg 19% DV.

Zucchini Corn Fritters

Prep: 15 mins **Cook:** 4 mins **Total:** 19 mins **Servings:** 24 **Yield:** 24 fritters

Ingredients

- 2 cups all-purpose flour
- 1 tablespoon baking powder
- ½ teaspoon cumin
- ½ cup sugar
- ½ teaspoon salt
- 1 pinch fresh ground black pepper
- 2 large eggs eggs, beaten
- 1 cup milk
- ¼ cup butter, melted
- 2 cups grated zucchini
- 1 ½ cups fresh corn, kernels cut from cob
- 1 cup finely shredded Cheddar cheese
- 1 quart oil for frying

Directions

Step 1

In a large bowl, stir together flour, baking powder, cumin, sugar, salt, and pepper.

Step 2

In a small bowl, whisk together eggs, milk, and butter. Whisk wet ingredients into dry ingredients. Stir in zucchini, corn, and cheese; mix well.

Step 3

Warm oil in a cast iron skillet over medium-high heat. Drop batter by the tablespoonful into hot oil. Fry until crisp and brown, turning once with tongs. Remove to paper towels.

Nutrition Facts

Per Serving:

143.7 calories; protein 3.6g 7% DV; carbohydrates 15g 5% DV; fat 8g 12% DV; cholesterol 26.3mg 9% DV; sodium 146mg 6% DV.

Mexican Shrimp Cocktail

Prep: 15 mins **Additional:** 3 hrs **Total:** 3 hrs 15 mins **Servings:** 6 **Yield:** 6 servings

Ingredients

- 2 pounds cooked shrimp, peeled and deveined
- 1 tablespoon crushed garlic
- ½ cup finely chopped red onion
- ¼ cup fresh cilantro, chopped
- 1 ½ cups tomato and clam juice cocktail
- ¼ cup ketchup
- ¼ cup fresh lime juice
- 1 teaspoon hot pepper sauce, or to taste
- ¼ cup prepared horseradish
- 1 pinch salt to taste
- 1 ripe avocado - peeled, pitted and chopped

Directions

Step 1

Place the shrimp in a large bowl. Stir garlic, red onion, and cilantro. Mix in tomato and clam juice cocktail, ketchup, lime juice, hot pepper sauce, and horseradish. Season with salt. Gently stir in avocado. Cover, and refrigerate 2 to 3 hours. Serve in one large bowl or ladle into individual bowls.

Nutrition Facts

Per Serving:

257.8 calories; protein 33.3g 67% DV; carbohydrates 15.8g 5% DV; fat 6.7g 10% DV; cholesterol 295.1mg 98% DV; sodium 710.6mg 28% DV.

Salsa

Prep: 10 mins **Total:** 10 mins **Servings:** 4 **Yield:** 4 cups

Ingredients

- 4 large tomatoes, chopped
- 1 onion, chopped
- ½ cup chopped fresh cilantro
- 3 cloves garlic, minced
- 1 tablespoon lime juice
- 1 tomatillo, diced
- salt to taste
- 1 jalapeno pepper, minced

Directions

Step 1

In a medium-size mixing bowl, combine tomatoes, onion, cilantro, garlic, lime juice, tomatillo, and salt to taste. Mix well. Add 1/2 of the jalapeno pepper, and taste. If you desire your salsa with more of a kick, add the remaining 1/2 jalapeno. If you are satisfied with the salsa's heat, do not add the remaining jalapeno pepper. Cover the salsa, and chill until ready to serve.

Nutrition Facts

Per Serving:

53.2 calories; protein 2.3g 5% DV; carbohydrates 11.7g 4% DV; fat 0.5g 1% DV; cholesterolmg; sodium 13.4mg 1% DV.

Old-Fashioned Italian Zucchini Fritters

Prep: 20 mins **Cook:** 15 mins **Total:** 35 mins **Servings:** 25 **Yield:** 25 fritters

Ingredients

- 6 large eggs eggs
- 3 eaches zucchinis, shredded
- 1 zucchini, diced
- 1 teaspoon salt
- ½ teaspoon ground black pepper
- 3 tablespoons grated Parmesan cheese
- ¼ cup chopped fresh basil
- 1 ½ cups all-purpose flour
- 2 cups vegetable oil for frying

Directions

Step 1

Beat the eggs in a mixing bowl with a wire whisk until smooth. Stir in the shredded and diced zucchini, then season with salt, pepper, Parmesan cheese, and basil. Add the flour a little at a time, stirring between additions until no dry lumps remain.

Step 2

Heat the oil in a large skillet to 375 degrees F (190 degrees C).

Step 3

Drop the batter into the hot oil by the spoonful a few at a time making sure not to overcrowd the oil. Cook until the fritters are golden brown on each side, about 4 minutes. Drain on a paper towel-lined plate before serving.

Nutrition Facts

Per Serving:

65.8 calories; protein 2.8g 6% DV; carbohydrates 6.5g 2% DV; fat 3.2g 5% DV; cholesterol 45.2mg 15% DV; sodium 121.1mg 5% DV.

Peach Pie

Prep: 1 hr **Cook:** 45 mins **Total:** 1 hr 45 mins **Servings:** 8 **Yield:** 1 - 9 inch pie

Ingredients

- 10 medium (2-1/2" dia) (approx 4 per lb)s fresh peaches, pitted and sliced
- ⅓ cup all-purpose flour
- 1 cup white sugar
- ¼ cup butter
- 1 recipe pastry for a 9 inch double crust pie

Directions

Step 1

Mix flour, sugar and butter into crumb stage.

Step 2

Place one crust in the bottom of a 9 inch pie plate. Line the shell with some sliced peaches. Sprinkle some of the butter mixture on top of the peaches, then put more peaches on top of the the crumb mixture. Continue layering until both the peaches and crumbs are gone.

Step 3

Top with lattice strips of pie crust.

Step 4

Bake at 350 degrees F (175 degrees C) for 45 minutes, or until crust is golden. Allow pie to cool before slicing. Best when eaten fresh.

Nutrition Facts

Per Serving:

424.9 calories; protein 3.4g 7% DV; carbohydrates 57g 18% DV; fat 20.7g 32% DV; cholesterol 15.3mg 5% DV; sodium 279.6mg 11% DV.

Strawberry Angel Food Dessert

Prep: 15 mins **Total:** 15 mins **Servings:** 18 **Yield:** 1 9x13 inch dish

Ingredients

- 1 (10 inch) angel food cake
- 2 (8 ounce) packages cream cheese, softened
- 1 cup white sugar
- 1 (8 ounce) container frozen whipped topping, thawed
- 1 quart fresh strawberries, sliced
- 1 (18 ounce) jar strawberry glaze

Directions

Step 1

Crumble the cake into a 9x13 inch dish.

Step 2

Beat the cream cheese and sugar in a medium bowl until light and fluffy. Fold in whipped topping. Mash the cake down with your hands and spread the cream cheese mixture over the cake.

Step 3

In a bowl, combine strawberries and glaze until strawberries are evenly coated. Spread over cream cheese layer. Chill until serving.

Nutrition Facts

Per Serving:

260.8 calories; protein 3.2g 6% DV; carbohydrates 36.3g 12% DV; fat 11g 17% DV; cholesterol 27.4mg 9% DV; sodium 241.8mg 10% DV.

Old-Fashioned Italian Zucchini Fritters

Prep: 20 mins **Cook:** 15 mins **Total:** 35 mins **Servings:** 25 **Yield:** 25 fritters

Ingredients

- 6 large eggs eggs
- 3 eaches zucchinis, shredded
- 1 zucchini, diced
- 1 teaspoon salt
- ½ teaspoon ground black pepper
- 3 tablespoons grated Parmesan cheese
- ¼ cup chopped fresh basil
- 1 ½ cups all-purpose flour
- 2 cups vegetable oil for frying

Directions

Step 1

Beat the eggs in a mixing bowl with a wire whisk until smooth. Stir in the shredded and diced zucchini, then season with salt, pepper, Parmesan cheese, and basil. Add the flour a little at a time, stirring between additions until no dry lumps remain.

Step 2

Heat the oil in a large skillet to 375 degrees F (190 degrees C).

Step 3

Drop the batter into the hot oil by the spoonful a few at a time making sure not to overcrowd the oil. Cook until the fritters are golden brown on each side, about 4 minutes. Drain on a paper towel-lined plate before serving.

Nutrition Facts

Per Serving:

65.8 calories; protein 2.8g 6% DV; carbohydrates 6.5g 2% DV; fat 3.2g 5% DV; cholesterol 45.2mg 15% DV; sodium 121.1mg 5% DV.

Vinegar Pickled Carrots

Prep: 10 mins **Cook:** 15 mins **Additional:** 12 hrs **Total:** 12 hrs 25 mins **Servings:** 32 **Yield:** 4 cups

Ingredients

- 1 cup distilled white vinegar
- 2 tablespoons white sugar
- 1 teaspoon salt
- ⅛ teaspoon ground black pepper
- ⅔ cup water
- 8 large carrots, diced

Directions

Step 1

In a medium saucepan, mix distilled white vinegar, white sugar, salt, pepper and water. Bring the mixture to a boil. Remove from heat and allow to cool slightly.

Step 2

Place the carrots in sterile containers. Cover with the vinegar solution. Seal the containers, refrigerate and marinate carrots 12 hours or overnight before serving.

Nutrition Facts

Per Serving:

10.6 calories; protein 0.2g; carbohydrates 2.5g 1% DV; fatg; cholesterolmg; sodium 85.1mg 3% DV.

Margaritas

Prep: 5 mins **Total:** 5 mins **Servings:** 4 **Yield:** 4 servings

Ingredients

- 1 (6 ounce) can frozen limeade concentrate
- 6 fluid ounces tequila
- 2 fluid ounces triple sec

Directions

Step 1

Fill blender with crushed ice. Pour in limeade concentrate, tequila and triple sec. Blend until smooth. Pour into glasses and serve.

Nutrition Facts

Per Serving:

286 calories; proteing; carbohydrates 40.6g 14% DV; fatg; cholesterolmg; sodium 1.4mg.

Quick and Easy Vegetable Soup

Servings: 6 Yield: 6 servings

Ingredients

- 1 (14 ounce) can chicken broth
- 1 (11.5 ounce) can tomato-vegetable juice cocktail
- 1 cup water
- 1 large potato, diced
- 2 carrot, (7-1/2")s carrots, sliced
- 2 stalks celery, diced
- 1 (14.5 ounce) can diced tomatoes
- 1 cup chopped fresh green beans
- 1 cup fresh corn kernels
- salt and pepper to taste
- Creole seasoning to taste

Directions

Step 1

In a large stock pot, combine broth, tomato juice, water, potatoes, carrots, celery, undrained chopped tomatoes, green beans, and corn. Season with salt, pepper and Creole seasoning. Bring to a boil and simmer for 30 minutes or until all vegetables are tender.

Nutrition Facts

Per Serving:

116.2 calories; protein 4g 8% DV; carbohydrates 24.3g 8% DV; fat 0.6g 1% DV; cholesterol 1.6mg 1% DV; sodium 639.5mg 26% DV.

Garden Tomato Salsa

Prep: 15 mins **Total:** 15 mins **Servings:** 10 **Yield:** 10 servings

Ingredients

- ½ sweet onion, chopped
- ½ green bell pepper, coarsely chopped
- ¼ cup fresh cilantro
- 5 slices pickled jalapeno peppers, or to taste
- 6 eaches fresh tomatoes, quartered
- 2 teaspoons olive oil

- 2 teaspoons red wine vinegar
- ½ lime, juiced
- ⅛ teaspoon salt

Directions

Step 1

Place onion, bell pepper, cilantro, and jalapeno peppers into a food processor. Pulse until finely chopped. Add tomatoes, and pulse just a few times until the tomatoes are coarsely chopped. Transfer to a bowl with a tight-fitting lid.

Step 2

In a separate bowl, whisk together olive oil, red wine vinegar, lime juice, and salt.

Step 3

Pour dressing over tomatoes, and stir well. Cover, and refrigerate for at least 1 hour.

Nutrition Facts

Per Serving:

29.9 calories; protein 1g 2% DV; carbohydrates 4.8g 2% DV; fat 1.2g 2% DV; cholesterolmg; sodium 67.9mg 3% DV.

Savory Garlic Marinated Steaks

Prep: 15 mins **Cook:** 15 mins **Additional:** 1 day **Total:** 1 day **Servings:** 2 **Yield:** 2 servings

Ingredients

- ½ cup balsamic vinegar
- ¼ cup soy sauce
- 3 tablespoons minced garlic
- 2 tablespoons honey
- 2 tablespoons olive oil
- 2 teaspoons ground black pepper
- 1 teaspoon Worcestershire sauce
- 1 teaspoon onion powder
- ½ teaspoon salt
- ½ teaspoon liquid smoke flavoring
- 1 pinch cayenne pepper
- 2 (1/2 pound) rib-eye steaks

Directions

Step 1

In a medium bowl, mix the vinegar, soy sauce, garlic, honey, olive oil, ground black pepper, Worcestershire sauce, onion powder, salt, liquid smoke, and cayenne pepper.

Step 2

Place steaks in a shallow glass dish with the marinade, and turn to coat. For optimum flavor, rub the liquid into the meat. Cover, and marinate in the refrigerator for 1 to 2 days.

Step 3

Preheat grill for medium-high to high heat.

Step 4

Lightly oil the grill grate. Grill steaks 7 minutes per side, or to desired doneness. Discard leftover marinade.

Cook's Note:

Aluminum foil can be used to keep food moist, cook it evenly, and make clean-up easier.

Nutrition Facts
Per Serving:

576.4 calories; protein 28.4g 57% DV; carbohydrates 36g 12% DV; fat 36g 55% DV; cholesterol 81.2mg 27% DV; sodium 2496.5mg 100% DV.

Stuffed Peppers

Prep: 20 mins **Cook:** 1 hr **Total:** 1 hr 20 mins **Servings:** 6 **Yield:** 6 servings

Ingredients

- 1 pound ground beef
- ½ cup uncooked long grain white rice
- 1 cup water
- 6 medium (blank)s green bell peppers
- 2 (8 ounce) cans tomato sauce
- 1 tablespoon Worcestershire sauce
- ¼ teaspoon garlic powder
- ¼ teaspoon onion powder
- ¼ teaspoon salt and pepper to taste
- 1 teaspoon Italian seasoning

Directions

Step 1

Preheat oven to 350 degrees F (175 degrees C).

Step 2

Place the rice and water in a saucepan, and bring to a boil. Reduce heat, cover, and cook 20 minutes. In a skillet over medium heat, cook the beef until evenly browned.

Step 3

Remove and discard the tops, seeds, and membranes of the bell peppers. Arrange peppers in a baking dish with the hollowed sides facing upward. (Slice the bottoms of the peppers if necessary so that they will stand upright.)

Step 4

In a bowl, mix the browned beef, cooked rice, 1 can tomato sauce, Worcestershire sauce, garlic powder, onion powder, salt, and pepper. Spoon an equal amount of the mixture into each hollowed pepper. Mix the remaining tomato sauce and Italian seasoning in a bowl, and pour over the stuffed peppers.

Step 5

Bake 1 hour in the preheated oven, basting with sauce every 15 minutes, until the peppers are tender.

Nutrition Facts

Per Serving:

247.7 calories; protein 16g 32% DV; carbohydrates 25.6g 8% DV; fat 9.4g 14% DV; cholesterol 45.9mg 15% DV; sodium 563.6mg 23% DV.

Easy Zucchini Fritters

Prep: 20 mins **Cook:** 5 mins **Additional:** 10 mins **Total:** 35 mins **Servings:** 4 **Yield:** 4 servings

Ingredients

- 1 ½ pounds zucchini, grated
- 1 teaspoon salt
- ¼ cup all-purpose flour
- ¼ cup grated Parmesan cheese
- 1 large egg, beaten
- 2 cloves garlic, minced
- 1 pinch kosher salt and ground black pepper to taste
- 2 tablespoons olive oil

Directions

Step 1

Toss zucchini and salt together in a large colander and place in sink to drain for 10 minutes.

Step 2

Put zucchini in the middle of a piece of cheesecloth; wrap cheesecloth around zucchini and squeeze to drain as much moisture from zucchini as possible.

Step 3

Mix flour, Parmesan cheese, egg, garlic, kosher salt, and pepper together in a large bowl. Stir in zucchini.

Step 4

Heat olive oil in a large skillet over medium-high heat.

Step 5

Scoop batter by the tablespoon into the hot skillet and fry until golden brown, about 2 minutes per side.

Nutrition Facts

Per Serving:

157 calories; protein 6.5g 13% DV; carbohydrates 12.5g 4% DV; fat 9.8g 15% DV; cholesterol 50.9mg 17% DV; sodium 792.9mg 32% DV.

Easy Garlic-Lemon Scallops

Prep: 10 mins **Cook:** 10 mins **Total:** 20 mins **Servings:** 6 **Yield:** 6 servings

Ingredients

- ¾ cup butter
- 3 tablespoons minced garlic
- 2 pounds large sea scallops
- 1 tcaspoon salt
- ⅛ teaspoon pepper
- 2 tablespoons fresh lemon juice

Directions

Step 1

Melt butter in a large skillet over medium-high heat. Stir in garlic, and cook for a few seconds until fragrant. Add scallops, and cook for several minutes on one side, then turn over, and continue cooking until firm and opaque.

Step 2

Remove scallops to a platter, then whisk salt, pepper, and lemon juice into butter. Pour sauce over scallops to serve.

Nutrition Facts

Per Serving:

408 calories; protein 38.5g 77% DV; carbohydrates 8.9g 3% DV; fat 24.4g 38% DV; cholesterol 152.4mg 51% DV; sodium 987.9mg 40% DV.

No-Noodle Zucchini Lasagna

Prep: 30 mins **Cook:** 1 hr **Total:** 1 hr 30 mins **Servings:** 8 **Yield:** 1 - 9x13 inch baking dish

Ingredients

- 2 large zucchini
- 1 tablespoon salt
- 1 pound ground beef
- 1 ½ teaspoons ground black pepper
- 1 small green bell pepper, diced
- 1 onion, diced
- 1 cup tomato paste
- 1 (16 ounce) can tomato sauce
- ¼ cup red wine
- 2 tablespoons chopped fresh basil

- 1 tablespoon chopped fresh oregano
- ¼ cup hot water as needed
- 1 egg
- 1 (15 ounce) container low-fat ricotta cheese
- 2 tablespoons chopped fresh parsley
- 1 (16 ounce) package frozen chopped spinach, thawed and drained
- 1 pound fresh mushrooms, sliced
- 8 ounces shredded mozzarella cheese
- 8 ounces grated Parmesan cheese

Directions

Step 1

Preheat oven to 325 degrees F (165 degrees C). Grease a deep 9x13 inch baking pan.

Step 2

Slice zucchini lengthwise into very thin slices. Sprinkle slices lightly with salt; set aside to drain in a colander.

Step 3

To prepare the meat sauce, cook and stir ground beef and black pepper in a large skillet over medium high heat for 5 minutes. Add in green pepper and onion; cook and stir until meat is no longer pink. Stir in tomato paste, tomato sauce, wine, basil, and oregano, adding a small amount of hot water if sauce is too thick. Bring to a boil; reduce heat and simmer sauce for about 20 minutes, stirring frequently.

Step 4

Meanwhile, stir egg, ricotta, and parsley together in a bowl until well combined.

Step 5

To assemble lasagna, spread 1/2 of the meat sauce into the bottom of prepared pan. Then layer 1/2 the zucchini slices, 1/2 the ricotta mixture, all of the spinach, followed by all of the mushrooms, then 1/2 the mozzarella cheese. Repeat by layering the remaining meat sauce, zucchini slices, ricotta mixture, and mozzarella. Spread Parmesan cheese evenly over the top; cover with foil.

Step 6

Bake for 45 minutes. Remove foil; raise oven temperature to 350 degrees F (175 degrees C), and bake an additional 15 minutes. Let stand for 5 minutes before serving.

Cook's Note

The lasagna can be assembled a day ahead and refrigerated until ready to bake. You may need to lengthen baking time.

Nutrition Facts

Per Serving:

494 calories; protein 41.3g 83% DV; carbohydrates 23.2g 8% DV; fat 27.3g 42% DV; cholesterol 117.7mg 39% DV; sodium 2199.7mg 88% DV.

Blueberry Pie

Prep: 15 mins **Cook:** 50 mins **Total:** 1 hr 5 mins **Servings:** 8 **Yield:** 1 pie

Ingredients

- ¾ cup white sugar
- 3 tablespoons cornstarch
- ¼ teaspoon salt
- ½ teaspoon ground cinnamon
- 4 cups fresh blueberries
- 1 recipe pastry for a 9 inch double crust pie
- 1 tablespoon butter

Directions

Step 1

Preheat oven to 375 degrees F (190 degrees C).

Step 2

Mix sugar, cornstarch, salt, and cinnamon, and sprinkle over blueberries.

Step 3

Line pie dish with one pie crust. Pour berry mixture into the crust, and dot with butter. Cut remaining pastry into 1/2 - 3/4 inch wide strips, and make lattice top. Crimp and flute edges.

Step 4

Bake pie on lower shelf of oven for about 50 minutes, or until crust is golden brown.

Nutrition Facts

Per Serving:

365.9 calories; protein 3.3g 7% DV; carbohydrates 52.6g 17% DV; fat 16.6g 26% DV; cholesterol 3.8mg 1% DV; sodium 317.7mg 13% DV.

Grilled Portobello with Basil Mayonnaise Sandwich

Prep: 10 mins **Cook:** 10 mins **Additional:** 5 mins **Total:** 25 mins **Servings:** 6 **Yield:** 6 sandwiches

Ingredients

- ⅓ cup balsamic vinegar
- ¼ cup olive oil
- 1 tablespoon minced garlic
- 6 mushrooms portobello mushroom caps
- ½ cup mayonnaise
- 1 tablespoon Dijon mustard

- 1 teaspoon lemon juice
- 2 tablespoons chopped fresh basil
- 6 eaches kaiser rolls, split, toasted
- 1 tablespoon butter
- 6 leaves lettuce
- 6 medium whole (2-3/5" dia) (blank)s tomato slices

Directions

Step 1

Preheat an outdoor grill for medium heat, and lightly oil the grate. Whisk together the balsamic vinegar, olive oil, and garlic in a small bowl.

Step 2

Arrange the portobello mushrooms gill-side up on a tray or baking sheet. Brush the mushrooms with some of the vinegar mixture, and allow to marinate for 3 to 5 minutes.

Step 3

Place the marinated mushrooms on the preheated grill, gill-side down. Grill mushrooms until tender, brushing both sides of the mushrooms with the remaining marinade, about 4 minutes on each side.

Step 4

Mix the mayonnaise, dijon mustard, lemon juice, and basil in a small bowl. Butter the toasted kaiser rolls, then spread with the mayonnaise mixture. Divide the mushrooms, lettuce, and tomato slices evenly to make 6 sandwiches.

Nutrition Facts

Per Serving:

411.9 calories; protein 8.3g 17% DV; carbohydrates 35.6g 12% DV; fat 27.7g 43% DV; cholesterol 12.1mg 4% DV; sodium 417.4mg 17% DV.

The Real Mojito

Prep: 10 mins **Total:** 10 mins **Servings:** 1 **Yield:** 1 cocktail

Ingredients

- 10 leaf (blank)s fresh mint leaves
- ½ lime, cut into 4 wedges
- 2 tablespoons white sugar, or to taste
- 1 cup ice cubes
- 1 ½ fluid ounces white rum
- ½ cup club soda

Directions

Step 1

Place mint leaves and 1 lime wedge into a sturdy glass. Use a muddler to crush the mint and lime to release the mint oils and lime juice. Add 2 more lime wedges and the sugar, and muddle again to release the lime juice. Do not strain the mixture. Fill the glass almost to the top with ice. Pour the rum over the ice, and fill the glass with carbonated water. Stir, taste, and add more sugar if desired. Garnish with the remaining lime wedge.

Nutrition Facts

Per Serving:

203.3 calories; protein 0.2g; carbohydrates 28.6g 10% DV; fat 0.1g; cholesterolmg; sodium 11.4mg.

Oven-Roasted Asparagus

Prep: 10 mins **Cook:** 15 mins **Total:** 25 mins **Servings:** 4 **Yield:** 4 servings

Ingredients

- 1 bunch thin asparagus spears, trimmed
- 3 tablespoons olive oil
- 1 ½ tablespoons grated Parmesan cheese
- 1 clove garlic, minced
- 1 teaspoon sea salt
- ½ teaspoon ground black pepper
- 1 tablespoon lemon juice

Directions

Step 1

Preheat an oven to 425 degrees F (220 degrees C).

Step 2

Place the asparagus into a mixing bowl, and drizzle with the olive oil. Toss to coat the spears, then sprinkle with Parmesan cheese, garlic, salt, and pepper. Arrange the asparagus onto a baking sheet in a single layer.

Step 3

Bake in the preheated oven until just tender, 12 to 15 minutes depending on thickness. Sprinkle with lemon juice just before serving.

Cook's Note

To remove woody ends, grab stalk of asparagus at either end and bend until it snaps. It will naturally snap where it starts to get tough.

Nutrition Facts

Per Serving:

123 calories; protein 3.3g 7% DV; carbohydrates 5.2g 2% DV; fat 10.8g 17% DV; cholesterol 1.7mg 1% DV; sodium 471.4mg 19% DV.

Yellow Squash Casserole

Prep: 20 mins **Cook:** 30 mins **Total:** 50 mins **Servings:** 10 **Yield:** 1 - 9x13 inch pan

Ingredients

- 4 cups sliced yellow squash
- ½ cup chopped onion
- 35 round crackers buttery round crackers, crushed
- 1 cup shredded Cheddar cheese
- 2 large eggs eggs, beaten
- ¾ cup milk
- ¼ cup butter, melted
- 1 teaspoon salt
- ground black pepper to taste
- 2 tablespoons butter

Directions

Step 1

Preheat oven to 400 degrees F (200 degrees C).

Step 2

Place squash and onion in a large skillet over medium heat. Pour in a small amount of water. Cover, and cook until squash is tender, about 5 minutes. Drain well, and place in a large bowl.

Step 3

In a medium bowl, mix together cracker crumbs and cheese. Stir half of the cracker mixture into the cooked squash and onions. In a small bowl, mix together eggs and milk, then add to squash mixture. Stir in 1/4 cup melted butter, and season with salt and pepper. Spread into a 9x13 inch baking dish. Sprinkle with remaining cracker mixture, and dot with 2 tablespoons butter.

Step 4

Bake in preheated oven for 25 minutes, or until lightly browned.

Nutrition Facts

Per Serving:

195.7 calories; protein 6.1g 12% DV; carbohydrates 10.3g 3% DV; fat 14.8g 23% DV; cholesterol 68.8mg 23% DV; sodium 463.5mg 19% DV.

Microwave Corn on the Cob

Cook: 5 mins **Total:** 5 mins **Servings:** 1 **Yield:** 1 serving

Ingredients

- 1 ear corn, husked and cleaned

Directions

Step 1

Wet a paper towel, and wring out. Wrap the ear of corn in the moist towel, and place on a dinner plate. Cook in the microwave for 5 minutes. Carefully remove paper towel, and enjoy!

Nutrition Facts

Per Serving:

123 calories; protein 4.6g 9% DV; carbohydrates 27.2g 9% DV; fat 1.7g 3% DV; cholesterolmg; sodium 21.5mg 1% DV.

Best Fried Green Tomatoes

Prep: 5 mins **Cook:** 15 mins **Total:** 20 mins **Servings:** 4 **Yield:** 4 servings

Ingredients

- 4 large green tomatoes
- 2 large eggs eggs
- ½ cup milk
- 1 cup all-purpose flour
- ½ cup cornmeal
- ½ cup bread crumbs
- 2 teaspoons coarse kosher salt
- ¼ teaspoon ground black pepper
- 1 quart vegetable oil for frying

Directions

Step 1

Slice tomatoes 1/2 inch thick. Discard the ends.

Step 2

Whisk eggs and milk together in a medium-size bowl. Scoop flour onto a plate. Mix cornmeal, bread crumbs and salt and pepper on another plate. Dip tomatoes into flour to coat. Then dip the tomatoes into milk and egg mixture. Dredge in breadcrumbs to completely coat.

Step 3

In a large skillet, pour vegetable oil (enough so that there is 1/2 inch of oil in the pan) and heat over a medium heat. Place tomatoes into the frying pan in batches of 4 or 5, depending on the size of your skillet. Do not crowd the tomatoes, they should not touch each other. When the tomatoes are browned, flip and fry them on the other side. Drain them on paper towels.

Nutrition Facts

Per Serving:

510 calories; protein 12.6g 25% DV; carbohydrates 56.3g 18% DV; fat 27g 42% DV; cholesterol 95.4mg 32% DV; sodium 1136mg 45% DV.

Balsamic Bruschetta

Prep: 15 mins **Total:** 15 mins **Servings:** 8 **Yield:** 8 servings

Ingredients

- 8 plum tomato (blank)s roma (plum) tomatoes, diced
- ⅓ cup chopped fresh basil
- ¼ cup shredded Parmesan cheese
- 2 cloves garlic, minced
- 1 tablespoon balsamic vinegar
- 1 teaspoon olive oil
- ¼ teaspoon kosher salt
- ¼ teaspoon freshly ground black pepper
- 1 loaf French bread, toasted and sliced

Directions

Step 1

In a bowl, toss together the tomatoes, basil, Parmesan cheese, and garlic. Mix in the balsamic vinegar, olive oil, kosher salt, and pepper. Serve on toasted bread slices.

Nutrition Facts

Per Serving:

194.1 calories; protein 8.3g 17% DV; carbohydrates 35.2g 11% DV; fat 2.5g 4% DV; cholesterol 2.2mg 1% DV; sodium 470.9mg 19% DV.

Crisp Pickled Green Beans

Prep: 1 hr **Cook:** 10 mins **Total:** 1 hr 10 mins **Servings:** 48 **Yield:** 6 - half pint jars

Ingredients

- 2 ½ pounds fresh green beans
- 2 ½ cups distilled white vinegar
- 2 cups water
- ¼ cup salt
- 1 clove garlic, peeled
- 1 bunch fresh dill weed
- ¾ teaspoon red pepper flakes

Directions

Step 1

Sterilize 6 (1/2 pint) jars with rings and lids and keep hot. Trim green beans to 1/4 inch shorter than your jars.

Step 2

In a large saucepan, stir together the vinegar, water and salt. Add garlic and bring to a rolling boil over high heat. In each jar, place 1 sprig of dill and 1/8 teaspoon of red pepper flakes. Pack green beans into the jars so they are standing on their ends.

Step 3

Ladle the boiling brine into the jars, filling to within 1/4 inch of the tops. Discard garlic. Seal jars with lids and rings. Place in a hot water bath so they are covered by 1 inch of water. Simmer but do not boil for 10 minutes to process. Cool to room temperature. Test jars for a good seal by pressing on the center of the lid. It should not move. Refrigerate any jars that do not seal properly. Let pickles ferment for 2 to 3 weeks before eating.

Nutrition Facts

Per Serving:

8.1 calories; protein 0.5g 1% DV; carbohydrates 1.8g 1% DV; fatg; cholesterolmg; sodium 2.1mg.

Best Ever Blueberry Cobbler

Prep: 20 mins **Cook:** 40 mins **Total:** 1 hr **Servings:** 6 **Yield:** 6 servings

Ingredients

- 3 cups fresh blueberries
- 3 tablespoons white sugar
- ⅓ cup orange juice
- ⅔ cup all-purpose flour
- ¼ teaspoon baking powder
- 1 pinch salt
- ½ cup butter, softened
- ½ cup white sugar
- 1 egg
- ½ teaspoon vanilla extract

Directions

Step 1

Preheat oven to 375 degrees F (190 degrees C).

Step 2

In an 8 inch square baking dish, mix blueberries, 3 tablespoons sugar, and orange juice. Set aside. In a small bowl, thoroughly mix flour, baking powder, and salt. Set aside.

Step 3

In a medium bowl, cream butter and 1/2 cup sugar until light and fluffy. Beat in egg and vanilla extract. Gradually add flour mixture, stirring just until ingredients are combined. Drop batter by rounded tablespoons over blueberry mixture. Try to cover as much of filling as possible.

Step 4

Bake in preheated oven for 35 to 40 minutes, until topping is golden brown and filling is bubbling.

Nutrition Facts

Per Serving:

335.5 calories; protein 3.3g 7% DV; carbohydrates 45.6g 15% DV; fat 16.6g 26% DV; cholesterol 71.7mg 24% DV; sodium 142.1mg 6% DV.

Homemade Tomato Sauce I

Prep: 30 mins **Cook:** 4 hrs **Total:** 4 hrs 30 mins **Servings:** 6 **Yield:** 3 cups

Ingredients

- 10 medium whole (2-3/5" dia) (blank)s ripe tomatoes
- 2 tablespoons olive oil
- 2 tablespoons butter
- 1 onion, chopped
- 1 green bell pepper, chopped
- 2 medium (blank)s carrots, chopped
- 4 cloves garlic, minced
- ¼ cup chopped fresh basil
- ¼ teaspoon Italian seasoning
- ¼ cup Burgundy wine
- 1 bay leaf
- 2 stalks celery
- 2 tablespoons tomato paste

Directions

Step 1

Bring a pot of water to a boil. Have ready a large bowl of iced water. Plunge whole tomatoes in boiling water until skin starts to peel, 1 minute. Remove with slotted spoon and place in ice bath. Let rest until cool enough to handle, then remove peel and squeeze out seeds. Chop 8 tomatoes and puree in blender or food processor. Chop remaining two tomatoes and set aside.

Step 2

In a large pot or Dutch oven over medium heat, cook onion, bell pepper, carrot and garlic in oil and butter until onion starts to soften, 5 minutes. Pour in pureed tomatoes. Stir in chopped tomato, basil, Italian seasoning and wine. Place bay leaf and whole celery stalks in pot. Bring to a boil, then reduce heat to low, cover and simmer 2 hours. Stir in tomato paste and simmer an additional 2 hours. Discard bay leaf and celery and serve.

Nutrition Facts

Per Serving:

148.6 calories; protein 2.9g 6% DV; carbohydrates 15g 5% DV; fat 8.9g 14% DV; cholesterol 10.2mg 3% DV; sodium 104.9mg 4% DV.

Blackberry Pie I

Prep: 40 mins **Cook:** 40 mins **Additional:** 1 hr **Total:** 2 hrs 20 mins **Servings:** 8 **Yield:** 1 9-inch pie

Ingredients

- 4 cups fresh blackberries
- ½ cup white sugar
- ½ cup all-purpose flour
- 1 recipe pastry for a 9 inch double crust pie
- 2 tablespoons milk
- ¼ cup white sugar

Directions

Step 1

Preheat oven to 425 degrees F (220 degrees C).

Step 2

Combine 3 1/2 cups berries with the sugar and flour. Spoon the mixture into an unbaked pie shell. Spread the remaining 1/2 cup berries on top of the sweetened berries, and cover with the top crust. Seal and crimp the edges, and cut vents in the top crust for steam to escape.

Step 3

Brush the top crust with milk, and sprinkle with 1/4 cup sugar.

Step 4

Bake in the preheated oven for 15 minutes. Reduce the temperature of the oven to 375 degrees F (190 degrees C), and bake for an additional 20 to 25 minutes, or until the filling is bubbly and the crust is golden brown. Cool on wire rack.

Nutrition Facts

Per Serving:

247.6 calories; protein 3.3g 7% DV; carbohydrates 42.1g 14% DV; fat 8g 12% DV; cholesterol 0.3mg; sodium 119.3mg 5% DV.

Summer Grilled Cabbage

Prep: 10 mins **Cook:** 30 mins **Total:** 40 mins **Servings:** 8 **Yield:** 8 servings

Ingredients

- 1 large head cabbage, cored and cut into 8 wedges
- 8 teaspoons butter
- ¼ cup water

- ½ teaspoon garlic powder, or to taste
- ½ teaspoon seasoned salt, or to taste
- 1 pinch ground black pepper to taste

Directions

Step 1

Preheat an outdoor grill for medium-high heat and lightly oil grate.

Step 2

Arrange the cabbage wedges into the bottom of a large metal baking dish. Pour the water into the dish. Place a teaspoon of butter on each cabbage wedge. Season liberally with garlic powder, seasoned salt, and pepper. Cover the dish with aluminum foil.

Step 3

Place the dish on the preheated grill; cook until cabbage is tender, about 30 minutes.

Nutrition Facts

Per Serving:

76 calories; protein 2.1g 4% DV; carbohydrates 9.3g 3% DV; fat 4.2g 7% DV; cholesterol 10.8mg 4% DV; sodium 114.6mg 5% DV.

Fresh Broccoli Salad

Prep: 15 mins **Cook:** 15 mins **Total:** 30 mins **Servings:** 9 **Yield:** 8 to 10 servings

Ingredients

- 2 heads fresh broccoli
- 1 red onion
- ½ pound bacon
- ¾ cup raisins
- ¾ cup sliced almonds
- 1 cup mayonnaise
- ½ cup white sugar
- 2 tablespoons white wine vinegar

Directions

Step 1

Place bacon in a deep skillet and cook over medium high heat until evenly brown. Cool and crumble.

Step 2

Cut the broccoli into bite-size pieces and cut the onion into thin bite-size slices. Combine with the bacon, raisins, your favorite nuts and mix well.

Step 3

To prepare the dressing, mix the mayonnaise, sugar and vinegar together until smooth. Stir into the salad, let chill and serve.

Perfect Summer Fruit Salad

Prep: 25 mins **Cook:** 5 mins **Additional:** 3 hrs **Total:** 3 hrs 30 mins **Servings:** 10 **Yield:** 10 servings

Ingredients

- ⅔ cup fresh orange juice
- ⅓ cup fresh lemon juice
- ⅓ cup packed brown sugar
- ½ teaspoon grated orange zest
- ½ teaspoon grated lemon zest
- 1 teaspoon vanilla extract
- 2 cups cubed fresh pineapple
- 2 cups strawberries, hulled and sliced
- 3 medium fruit, without skins kiwi fruit, peeled and sliced
- 3 medium (7" to 7-7/8" long)s bananas, sliced
- 2 fruit, (2-5/8" dia, sphere)s oranges, peeled and sectioned
- 1 cup seedless grapes
- 2 cups blueberries

Directions

Step 1

Bring orange juice, lemon juice, brown sugar, orange zest, and lemon zest to a boil in a saucepan over medium-high heat. Reduce heat to medium-low, and simmer until slightly thickened, about 5 minutes. Remove from heat, and stir in vanilla extract. Set aside to cool.

Step 2

Layer the fruit in a large, clear glass bowl in this order: pineapple, strawberries, kiwi fruit, bananas, oranges, grapes, and blueberries. Pour the cooled sauce over the fruit. Cover and refrigerate for 3 to 4 hours before serving.

Nutrition Facts

Per Serving:

155 calories; protein 1.8g 4% DV; carbohydrates 39g 13% DV; fat 0.6g 1% DV; cholesterolmg; sodium 4.7mg.

Stuffed Zucchini

Prep: 10 mins **Cook:** 1 hr **Total:** 1 hr 10 mins **Servings:** 4 **Yield:** 4 servings

Ingredients

- 3 medium (blank)s zucchini
- 1 pound pork sausage
- 1 cup dry bread crumbs
- 1 clove garlic, minced
- 1 (32 ounce) jar spaghetti sauce
- ½ cup grated Parmesan cheese
- ½ cup shredded mozzarella cheese

Directions

Step 1

Preheat oven to 350 degrees F (175 degrees C).

Step 2

Trim stems from zucchini and slice lengthwise. Scoop out seeds and put in a bowl. Mix seeds with sausage, garlic, bread crumbs, and Parmesan cheese. Stuff squash with sausage mixture and place in a 9x13 inch baking pan. Pour spaghetti sauce over the top and cover the pan with foil.

Step 3

Bake in preheated oven until sausage is browned and cooked through, about 45 minutes. Remove foil and cover with mozzarella cheese. Return to the oven and cook until cheese is melted, about 15 minutes more.

Nutrition Facts

Per Serving:

878.4 calories; protein 29.1g 58% DV; carbohydrates 58.2g 19% DV; fat 58.4g 90% DV; cholesterol 99.5mg 33% DV; sodium 2118mg 85% DV.

Grilled Sea Bass

Prep: 20 mins **Cook:** 20 mins **Total:** 40 mins **Servings:** 6 **Yield:** 6 servings

Ingredients

- ¼ teaspoon garlic powder
- ¼ teaspoon onion powder
- ¼ teaspoon paprika
- ¼ teaspoon lemon pepper to taste
- ¼ teaspoon sea salt to taste
- 2 pounds sea bass
- 3 tablespoons butter
- 2 large cloves garlic, chopped
- 1 tablespoon chopped Italian flat leaf parsley
- 1 ½ tablespoons extra virgin olive oil

Directions

Step 1

Preheat grill for high heat.

Step 2

In a small bowl, stir together the garlic powder, onion powder, paprika, lemon pepper, and sea salt. Sprinkle seasonings onto the fish.

Step 3

In a small saucepan over medium heat, melt the butter with the garlic and parsley. Remove from heat when the butter has melted, and set aside.

Step 4

Lightly oil grill grate. Grill fish for 7 minutes, then turn and drizzle with butter. Continue cooking for 7 minutes, or until easily flaked with a fork. Drizzle with olive oil before serving.

Nutrition Facts

Per Serving:

231.6 calories; protein 28.2g 56% DV; carbohydrates 0.8g; fat 12.2g 19% DV; cholesterol 77.9mg 26% DV; sodium 237mg 10% DV.

Garlic Chicken Stir Fry

Servings: 4 **Yield:** 4 servings

Ingredients

- 2 tablespoons peanut oil
- 6 cloves garlic, minced
- 1 teaspoon grated fresh ginger
- 1 bunch green onions, chopped
- 1 teaspoon salt
- 1 pound boneless skinless chicken breasts, cut into strips
- 2 medium (2-1/2" dia)s onions, thinly sliced
- 1 cup sliced cabbage
- 1 red bell pepper, thinly sliced
- 2 cups sugar snap peas
- 1 cup chicken broth
- 2 tablespoons soy sauce
- 2 tablespoons white sugar
- 2 tablespoons cornstarch

Directions

Step 1

Heat peanut oil in a wok or large skillet. When oil begins to smoke, quickly stir in 2 cloves minced garlic, ginger root, green onions and salt. Stir fry until onion becomes translucent, about 2 minutes. Add chicken and stir until opaque, about 3 minutes. Add remaining 4 cloves minced garlic and stir. Add sweet onions, cabbage, bell pepper, peas and 1/2 cup of the broth/water and cover.

Step 2

In a small bowl, mix the remaining 1/2 cup broth/water, soy sauce, sugar and cornstarch. Add sauce mixture to wok/skillet and stir until chicken and vegetables are coated with the thickened sauce. Serve immediately, over hot rice if desired.

Nutrition Facts

Per Serving:

337.3 calories; protein 31.7g 63% DV; carbohydrates 32.3g 10% DV; fat 8.6g 13% DV; cholesterol 67.1mg 22% DV; sodium 1363.8mg 55% DV.

Strawberry Pie II

Servings: 8 Yield: 1 9-inch pie

Ingredients

- 1 (9 inch) pie crust, baked
- 1 quart fresh strawberries
- 1 cup white sugar
- 3 tablespoons cornstarch
- ¾ cup water
- ½ cup heavy whipping cream

Directions

Step 1

Arrange half of strawberries in baked pastry shell. Mash remaining berries and combine with sugar in a medium saucepan. Place saucepan over medium heat and bring to a boil, stirring frequently.

Step 2

In a small bowl, whisk together cornstarch and water. Gradually stir cornstarch mixture into boiling strawberry mixture. Reduce heat and simmer mixture until thickened, about 10 minutes, stirring constantly. Pour mixture over berries in pastry shell. Chill for several hours before serving. In a small bowl, whip cream until soft peaks form. Serve each slice of pie with a dollop of whipped cream.

Nutrition Facts

Per Serving:

265 calories; protein 1.5g 3% DV; carbohydrates 41.9g 14% DV; fat 10.9g 17% DV; cholesterol 20.4mg 7% DV; sodium 109.3mg 4% DV.

Summertime Sweet Pickles

Prep: 10 mins **Additional:** 21 hrs 30 mins **Total:** 21 hrs 40 mins **Servings:** 8 **Yield:** 1 quart

Ingredients

- 1 cup apple cider vinegar
- ⅛ cup salt
- 1 cup white sugar
- ¼ teaspoon ground turmeric
- ½ teaspoon mustard seed
- 2 pounds cucumbers
- 2 medium (blank)s sweet onions

Directions

Step 1

In a small saucepan at medium-high heat, combine cider vinegar, salt, sugar, tumeric and mustard seed. Bring to a boil and let cook for 5 more minutes.

Step 2

Meanwhile, slice cucumbers and onion. Loosely pack the vegetables in a 1-quart canning jar or other similarly sized container. Pour hot liquid over the vegetables in the container. Refrigerate for 24 hours and enjoy! Keep refrigerated.

Nutrition Facts

Per Serving:

140.5 calories; protein 1.3g 3% DV; carbohydrates 33.5g 11% DV; fat 0.3g 1% DV; cholesterolmg; sodium 6.1mg.

Tomato Mozzarella Salad

Prep: 10 mins **Total:** 10 mins **Servings:** 6 **Yield:** 6 servings

Ingredients

- 3 large tomatoes, sliced
- 8 ounces mozzarella cheese, sliced
- ¼ cup olive oil
- ¼ cup balsamic vinegar
- ¼ teaspoon salt
- ⅛ teaspoon ground black pepper
- ¼ cup minced fresh basil

Directions

Step 1

Place tomato slices, alternating with mozzarella slices, on a large serving platter.

Step 2

Combine oil, balsamic vinegar, salt, and pepper in a jar with a tight-fitting lid; shake well. Drizzle over tomatoes and mozzarella; sprinkle with basil.

Nutrition Facts

Per Serving:

199 calories; protein 10.1g 20% DV; carbohydrates 6.2g 2% DV; fat 15.2g 23% DV; cholesterol 24.2mg 8% DV; sodium 338.3mg 14% DV.

Easy Stuffed Zucchini

Prep: 20 mins **Cook:** 50 mins **Total:** 1 hr 10 mins **Servings:** 4 **Yield:** 4 servings

Ingredients

- ½ pound ground beef
- 1 large zucchini, ends trimmed
- ½ cup bread crumbs
- 2 cloves garlic, minced
- 1 (16 ounce) jar spaghetti sauce
- ½ (6 ounce) can sliced black olives, drained
- ½ cup grated Parmesan cheese
- 1 cup shredded mozzarella cheese

Directions

Step 1

Preheat oven to 350 degrees F (175 degrees C).

Step 2

Cook and stir the ground beef in a skillet over medium heat until the meat is browned, breaking the beef up into crumbles as it cooks, about 10 minutes. Drain off excess fat, and transfer the beef into a mixing bowl. Slice the zucchini in half the long way, and use a spoon to scoop out the flesh, leaving a 1/2-inch thick shell all around the zucchini. Chop the scooped-out zucchini flesh, and add to mixing bowl. Stir in the bread crumbs, garlic, spaghetti sauce, black olives, and Parmesan cheese; mix the stuffing well. Lightly stuff both halves of the zucchini with the meat mixture. Place the zucchini halves into a baking dish, and cover tightly with foil.

Step 3

Bake in the preheated oven for 45 minutes, remove from oven, and remove the foil. Sprinkle 1/2 cup of shredded mozzarella cheese over each zucchini half. Move an oven rack to within 6 inches of the oven broiler's heat source, turn on the broiler, and broil the zucchini until the mozzarella cheese is browned and bubbling, about 5 minutes.

Nutrition Facts

Per Serving:

405.4 calories; protein 25.2g 50% DV; carbohydrates 30.9g 10% DV; fat 20.1g 31% DV; cholesterol 63.4mg 21% DV; sodium 1112.4mg 45% DV.

Red Skinned Potato Salad

Prep: 1 hr **Additional:** 1 hr **Total:** 2 hrs **Servings:** 12 **Yield:** 12 servings

Ingredients

- 2 pounds clean, scrubbed new red potatoes
- 6 large eggs eggs
- 1 pound bacon
- 1 onion, finely chopped
- 1 stalk celery, finely chopped
- 2 cups mayonnaise
- salt and pepper to taste

Directions

Step 1

Bring a large pot of salted water to a boil. Add potatoes and cook until tender but still firm, about 15 minutes. Drain and set in the refrigerator to cool.

Step 2

Place eggs in a saucepan and cover with cold water. Bring water to a boil and immediately remove from heat. Cover and let eggs stand in hot water for 10 to 12 minutes. Remove from hot water, cool, peel and chop.

Step 3

Place bacon in a large, deep skillet. Cook over medium high heat until evenly brown. Drain, crumble and set aside.

Step 4

Chop the cooled potatoes, leaving skin on. Add to a large bowl, along with the eggs, bacon, onion and celery. Add mayonnaise, salt and pepper to taste. Chill for an hour before serving.

Nutrition Facts

Per Serving:

429.6 calories; protein 9.5g 19% DV; carbohydrates 16.2g 5% DV; fat 36.9g 57% DV; cholesterol 120.6mg 40% DV; sodium 535.8mg 21% DV.

Unbelievable Chicken

Prep: 15 mins **Cook:** 20 mins **Additional:** 8 hrs 25 mins **Total:** 9 hrs **Servings:** 6 **Yield:** 6 servings

Ingredients

- ¼ cup cider vinegar

- 3 tablespoons prepared coarse-ground mustard
- 3 cloves garlic, peeled and minced
- 1 lime, juiced
- ½ lemon, juiced
- ½ cup brown sugar
- 1 ½ teaspoons salt
- 1 teaspoon ground black pepper to taste
- 6 tablespoons olive oil
- 6 breast half, bone and skin removed (blank)s skinless, boneless chicken breast halves

Directions

Step 1

In a large glass bowl, mix the cider vinegar, mustard, garlic, lime juice, lemon juice, brown sugar, salt, and pepper. Whisk in the olive oil. Place chicken in the mixture. Cover, and marinate 8 hours, or overnight.

Step 2

Preheat an outdoor grill for high heat.

Step 3

Lightly oil the grill grate. Place chicken on the prepared grill, and cook 6 to 8 minutes per side, until juices run clear. Discard marinade.

Nutrition Facts

Per Serving:

337.1 calories; protein 24.8g 50% DV; carbohydrates 22.4g 7% DV; fat 16.4g 25% DV; cholesterol 67.1mg 22% DV; sodium 735.5mg 29% DV.

Fried Stuffed Squash Blossoms

Prep: 30 mins **Cook:** 15 mins **Additional:** 30 mins **Total:** 1 hr 15 mins **Servings:** 12 **Yield:** 12 filled squash blossoms

Ingredients

- 12 flowers fresh zucchini blossoms
- ¾ cup soft goat cheese at room temperature
- 1 egg yolk
- ¼ cup shredded Gruyere cheese
- 1 pinch freshly ground black pepper, or to taste
- 1 pinch cayenne pepper

Batter:

- 1 cup self-rising flour
- ½ cup cornstarch
- ¼ cup ice-cold water, or as needed

- 2 cups vegetable oil for frying
- 1 teaspoon all-purpose flour, or as needed

Directions

Step 1

Bring a pot of lightly salted water to a boil. Prepare a large bowl of ice-cold water. Drop squash blossoms into the boiling water until slightly wilted, 30 to 45 seconds; transfer immediately into the cold water to chill. Remove to paper towels to drain.

Step 2

Mix goat cheese, egg yolk, Gruyere cheese, black pepper, and cayenne pepper together in a bowl; stir until smooth. Spoon filling into a heavy, resealable 1-quart plastic bag, squeeze out the air, and seal the bag. Cut a small corner off the bag.

Step 3

Gently insert the cut corner of the bag all the way to the bottom of the open end of a blossom and pipe about 1 tablespoon of filling inside. Pick up petals and drape them up over the filling, covering filling completely. Fold any excess petals over the top of the filled blossom to keep them out of the way. Refrigerate filled squash blossoms until cheese is set and firm, at least 30 minutes.

Step 4

Combine self-rising flour and cornstarch in a mixing bowl; whisk in ice-cold water, a little at a time, until batter is smooth and has the thickness of pancake batter.

Step 5

Pour vegetable oil to a depth of 1 inch into a heavy skillet (such as a cast iron pan) and place over medium heat. Heat oil until a thermometer placed into the oil, not touching the bottom, reads 350 degrees F (175 degrees C). A drop of batter carefully dripped into the oil should sizzle immediately.

Step 6

Remove squash blossoms from refrigerator and dust lightly with all-purpose flour on all sides. Shake off excess flour and dip blossoms in batter. Let excess batter drip off.

Step 7

Gently lay coated squash blossoms in the hot oil on their sides; cook about 6 at a time until pale golden brown, 1 minute on the first side and 30 seconds to 1 minute on the remaining sides. Let cool slightly before serving.

Chef's Note:

Use shredded Gruyere, Cheddar, Manchego, or any other firm cheese in the filling.

Nutrition Facts

Per Serving:

156.2 calories; protein 5g 10% DV; carbohydrates 13.3g 4% DV; fat 9.1g 14% DV; cholesterol 30.7mg 10% DV; sodium 214.3mg 9% DV.

Savory Garlic Marinated Steaks

Prep: 15 mins **Cook:** 15 mins **Additional:** 1 day **Total:** 1 day **Servings:** 2 **Yield:** 2 servings

Ingredients

- ½ cup balsamic vinegar
- ¼ cup soy sauce
- 3 tablespoons minced garlic
- 2 tablespoons honey
- 2 tablespoons olive oil
- 2 teaspoons ground black pepper
- 1 teaspoon Worcestershire sauce
- 1 teaspoon onion powder
- ½ teaspoon salt
- ½ teaspoon liquid smoke flavoring
- 1 pinch cayenne pepper
- 2 (1/2 pound) rib-eye steaks

Directions

Step 1

In a medium bowl, mix the vinegar, soy sauce, garlic, honey, olive oil, ground black pepper, Worcestershire sauce, onion powder, salt, liquid smoke, and cayenne pepper.

Step 2

Place steaks in a shallow glass dish with the marinade, and turn to coat. For optimum flavor, rub the liquid into the meat. Cover, and marinate in the refrigerator for 1 to 2 days.

Step 3

Preheat grill for medium-high to high heat.

Step 4

Lightly oil the grill grate. Grill steaks 7 minutes per side, or to desired doneness. Discard leftover marinade.

Cook's Note:

Aluminum foil can be used to keep food moist, cook it evenly, and make clean-up easier.

Nutrition Facts
Per Serving:

576.4 calories; protein 28.4g 57% DV; carbohydrates 36g 12% DV; fat 36g 55% DV; cholesterol 81.2mg 27% DV; sodium 2496.5mg 100% DV.

Cherry Pie Filling

Prep: 25 mins **Cook:** 15 mins **Total:** 40 mins **Servings:** 6 **Yield:** 4 cups

Ingredients

- 4 cups pitted tart red cherries
- 1 cup white sugar
- ¼ cup cornstarch

Directions

Step 1

Place cherries into a saucepan over medium heat, and cover the pan; heat cherries until they release their juice and come to a simmer, 10 to 15 minutes. Stir often.

Step 2

In a bowl, whisk the sugar with cornstarch until smooth; pour the mixture into the hot cherries and juice, and thoroughly combine. Return to low heat, bring to a simmer, and cook until the filling has thickened, about 2 minutes; remove from heat, let cool, and use as pie filling.

Nutrition Facts

Per Serving:

218.9 calories; protein 1.2g 2% DV; carbohydrates 54.2g 18% DV; fat 0.9g 1% DV; cholesterolmg; sodium 0.5mg.

Greek Chicken

Prep: 15 mins **Cook:** 30 mins **Additional:** 8 hrs **Total:** 8 hrs 45 mins **Servings:** 8 **Yield:** 8 servings

Ingredients

- ½ cup olive oil
- 3 cloves garlic, chopped
- 1 tablespoon chopped fresh rosemary
- 1 tablespoon chopped fresh thyme
- 1 tablespoon chopped fresh oregano
- 2 fruit, without seeds lemons, juiced
- 1 (4 pound) chicken, cut into pieces

Directions

Step 1

In a glass dish, mix the olive oil, garlic, rosemary, thyme, oregano, and lemon juice. Place the chicken pieces in the mixture, cover, and marinate in the refrigerator 8 hours or overnight.

Step 2

Preheat grill for high heat.

Step 3

Lightly oil the grill grate. Place chicken on the grill, and discard the marinade. Cook chicken pieces up to 15 minutes per side, until juices run clear. Smaller pieces will not take as long.

Nutrition Facts

Per Serving:

412.4 calories; protein 31.1g 62% DV; carbohydrates 3.5g 1% DV; fat 30.7g 47% DV; cholesterol 97.1mg 32% DV; sodium 94.6mg 4% DV.

Burger or Hot Dog Buns

Prep: 20 mins **Cook:** 10 mins **Additional:** 1 hr **Total:** 1 hr 30 mins **Servings:** 12 **Yield:** 1 dozen

Ingredients

- 1 cup milk
- ½ cup water
- ¼ cup butter
- 4 ½ cups all-purpose flour
- 1 (.25 ounce) package instant yeast
- 2 tablespoons white sugar
- 1 ½ teaspoons salt
- 1 egg

Directions

Step 1

In a small saucepan, heat milk, water and butter until very warm, 120 degrees F (50 degrees C).

Step 2

In a large bowl, mix together 1 3/4 cup flour, yeast, sugar and salt. Mix milk mixture into flour mixture, and then mix in egg. Stir in the remaining flour, 1/2 cup at a time, beating well after each addition. When the dough has pulled together, turn it out onto a lightly floured surface, and knead until smooth and elastic, about 8 minutes.

Step 3

Divide dough into 12 equal pieces. Shape into smooth balls, and place on a greased baking sheet. Flatten slightly. Cover, and let rise for 30 to 35 minutes.

Step 4

Bake at 400 degrees F (200 degrees C) for 10 to 12 minutes, or until golden brown.

Step 5

For Hot Dog Buns: Shape each piece into a 6x4 inch rectangle. Starting with the longer side, roll up tightly, and pinch edges and ends to seal. Let rise about 20 to 25 minutes. Bake as above. These buns are pretty big. I usually make 16 instead of 12.

Nutrition Facts

Per Serving:

230.4 calories; protein 6.3g 13% DV; carbohydrates 39.1g 13% DV; fat 5.1g 8% DV; cholesterol 27.3mg 9% DV; sodium 333.6mg 13% DV.

Rhubarb Jam

Prep: 25 mins **Cook:** 45 mins **Total:** 1 hr 10 mins **Servings:** 32 **Yield:** 2 pints

Ingredients

- 2 ½ pounds fresh rhubarb, chopped
- 2 cups white sugar
- 2 teaspoons grated orange zest
- ⅓ cup orange juice
- ½ cup water

Directions

Step 1

In a saucepan, combine the rhubarb, sugar, orange zest, orange juice and water. Bring to a boil, then cook over medium-low heat for 45 minutes, stirring occasionally, or until thick. It will thicken more as it cools.

Step 2

Ladle into hot sterile jars, and seal with lids and rings. Store opened jars in the refrigerator.

Nutrition Facts

Per Serving:

57.1 calories; protein 0.3g 1% DV; carbohydrates 14.4g 5% DV; fat 0.1g; cholesterolmg; sodium 1.6mg.

Fresh Tomato Salsa

Prep: 10 mins **Additional:** 1 hr **Total:** 1 hr 10 mins **Servings:** 4 **Yield:** 4 servings

Ingredients

- 3 medium whole (2-3/5" dia) (blank)s tomatoes, chopped
- ½ cup finely diced onion
- 5 eaches serrano chiles, finely chopped
- ½ cup chopped fresh cilantro
- 1 teaspoon salt
- 2 teaspoons lime juice

Directions

Step 1

In a medium bowl, stir together tomatoes, onion, chili peppers, cilantro, salt, and lime juice. Chill for one hour in the refrigerator before serving.

Nutrition Facts

Per Serving:

51.5 calories; protein 2.1g 4% DV; carbohydrates 9.7g 3% DV; fat 0.2g; cholesterolmg; sodium 592.1mg 24% DV.

Pesto Pasta Caprese Salad

Prep: 10 mins **Cook:** 10 mins **Total:** 20 mins **Servings:** 6 **Yield:** 6 servings

Ingredients

- 1 ½ cups rotini pasta
- 3 tablespoons pesto, or to taste
- 1 tablespoon extra-virgin olive oil
- ¼ teaspoon salt, or to taste
- ¼ teaspoon granulated garlic
- ⅛ teaspoon ground black pepper
- ½ cup halved grape tomatoes
- ½ cup small (pearlini) fresh mozzarella balls
- 2 leaves fresh basil leaves, finely shredded

Directions

Step 1

Bring a large pot of lightly salted water to a boil; cook the rotini at a boil until tender yet firm to the bite, about 8 minutes; drain.

Step 2

Mix pesto, olive oil, salt, granulated garlic, and black pepper in a bowl; add rotini. Toss to coat. Fold in tomatoes, mozzarella, and fresh basil.

Nutrition Facts

Per Serving:

168.6 calories; protein 6.1g 12% DV; carbohydrates 17.1g 6% DV; fat 8.3g 13% DV; cholesterol 10.4mg 4% DV; sodium 173.1mg 7% DV.

Stuffed Peppers My Way

Prep: 20 mins **Cook:** 40 mins **Total:** 1 hr **Servings:** 2 **Yield:** 2 servings

Ingredients

- 1 cup water
- ½ cup uncooked Arborio rice
- 2 medium (blank)s green bell peppers, halved and seeded
- 1 tablespoon olive oil
- 2 medium (4-1/8" long)s green onions, thinly sliced
- 1 teaspoon dried basil
- 1 teaspoon Italian seasoning
- 1 teaspoon salt
- 1 pinch ground black pepper
- 1 tomato, diced
- ½ cup crumbled feta cheese

Directions

Step 1

Preheat oven to 400 degrees F (200 degrees C). Lightly grease a baking sheet.

Step 2

In a medium saucepan, bring water to a boil. Stir in the rice. Reduce heat, cover, and simmer for 20 minutes. Remove from heat, and set aside.

Step 3

Place the peppers cut-side down on the prepared baking sheet. Roast 25 to 30 minutes in the preheated oven, or until tender and skin starts to brown.

Step 4

While the peppers are roasting, heat oil in a medium skillet over medium-high heat. Cook the onions, basil, Italian seasoning, salt, and pepper in oil for 2 to 3 minutes. Stir in the tomato, and cook for 5 minutes. Spoon in the cooked rice, and stir until heated through. Remove from heat, mix in the feta cheese, and spoon the mixture into the pepper halves.

Step 5

Return to the oven for 5 minutes. Serve immediately.

Nutrition Facts

Per Serving:

384.8 calories; protein 10.8g 22% DV; carbohydrates 52.6g 17% DV; fat 15.2g 23% DV; cholesterol 33.4mg 11% DV; sodium 1594.5mg 64% DV.

Connie's Zucchini "Crab" Cakes

Prep: 20 mins **Cook:** 10 mins **Total:** 30 mins **Servings:** 5 **Yield:** 4 to 6 servings

Ingredients

- 2 ½ cups grated zucchini
- 1 egg, beaten
- 2 tablespoons butter, melted
- 1 cup seasoned bread crumbs
- ¼ cup minced onion
- 1 teaspoon Old Bay Seasoning TM
- ¼ cup all-purpose flour
- ½ cup vegetable oil for frying

Directions

Step 1

In a large bowl, combine zucchini, egg, and butter or margarine. Stir in seasoned crumbs, minced onion, and seasoning. Mix well.

Step 2

Shape mixture into patties. Dredge in flour.

Step 3

In a medium skillet, heat oil over medium high heat until hot. Fry patties in oil until golden brown on both sides.

Nutrition Facts

Per Serving:

195.7 calories; protein 5.6g 11% DV; carbohydrates 23.2g 8% DV; fat 9.1g 14% DV; cholesterol 49.4mg 17% DV; sodium 319.9mg 13% DV.

Cuban Mojito

Prep: 10 mins **Total:** 10 mins **Servings:** 2 **Yield:** 2 servings

Ingredients

- 2 teaspoons white sugar
- 1 lime, cut into 4 wedges
- 4 sprigs fresh mint
- ½ cup white rum
- 2 cups club soda
- 2 cups crushed ice
- 2 wedges lime, as garnish

Directions

Step 1

Place 1 teaspoon of sugar into each of two 12 ounce glasses. Squeeze the juice from a lime wedge into each glass, drop in the wedge, and add 2 sprigs of mint. Use a spoon or muddler to mash the sugar, lime juice, and mint together in the bottom of the glasses. Fill each glass about half full with crushed ice. Pour 1/4 cup rum into each glass. Fill the glasses with club soda, stir, and garnish with additional lime wedges.

Nutrition Facts

Per Serving:

158 calories; protein 0.4g 1% DV; carbohydrates 8.5g 3% DV; fat 0.1g; cholesterolmg; sodium 13.2mg 1% DV.

Enchiladas Suizas

Prep: 45 mins **Cook:** 20 mins **Total:** 1 hr 5 mins **Servings:** 6 **Yield:** 6 servings

Ingredients

- 2 tablespoons butter
- ⅔ cup chopped Spanish onion
- 2 tablespoons all-purpose flour
- 1 ½ cups chicken broth
- 1 cup chopped green chile peppers

- 1 clove garlic, minced
- ¾ teaspoon salt
- 1 dash ground cumin
- 12 (8 inch) corn tortillas
- 1 quart canola oil for frying
- 1 cup shredded Monterey Jack cheese
- 1 cup shredded mild Cheddar cheese
- 2 cups shredded, cooked chicken breast meat
- 1 cup heavy cream
- ¼ cup chopped green onion
- ½ cup sliced green olives
- 1 pint cherry tomatoes

Directions

Step 1

Prepare salsa verde: Melt butter in saucepan over medium heat. Saute the onion until soft. Stir in the flour. Add the broth, then add the chiles, garlic, salt, and cumin. Simmer about 15 minutes to blend flavors, then set aside. Preheat oven to 350 degrees F (175 degrees C.)

Step 2

In a heavy skillet, lightly fry tortillas in shallow oil, being careful not to make them too crisp to roll. Combine the cheeses and keep 1/2 cup aside for topping. Dip each tortilla in salsa verde (both sides.) Place 2 heaping tablespoons chicken and about 2 tablespoons cheese down the center of each; roll and place seam side down in a shallow dish.

Step 3

After all the rolled tortillas are in the dish, spoon additional salsa verde over them and then cover evenly with heavy cream. Sprinkle with remaining 1/2 cup cheese mixture, and with the green onions.

Step 4

Bake uncovered in preheated oven for 20 minutes. Serve immediately, garnished with the olives, cherry tomatoes, and with additional salsa on the side.

Cook's Note:

Black olives can be used in place of the green olives, if desired.

Nutrition Facts

Per Serving:

737 calories; protein 28.5g 57% DV; carbohydrates 42.3g 14% DV; fat 52.1g 80% DV; cholesterol 136.1mg 45% DV; sodium 977.4mg 39% DV.

Pickled Squash

Prep: 4 hrs **Cook:** 5 mins **Total:** 4 hrs 5 mins **Servings:** 4 **Yield:** 4 pint jars

Ingredients

- ¼ cup salt
- 2 ½ pounds young yellow squash and zucchini, sliced into rounds
- 1 green bell pepper, seeded and sliced into strips
- 2 small onions, thinly sliced
- 2 ¼ cups white sugar
- 2 cups distilled white vinegar
- 2 teaspoons mustard seed
- 1 teaspoon ground turmeric
- 1 teaspoon celery seed

Directions

Step 1

In a large non-aluminum pot, combine the squash, bell pepper, and onions. Cover with salt, and let stand for 2 hours to release the liquids. Stir occasionally.

Step 2

Just before the 2 hours are up, combine the sugar, vinegar, mustard seed, turmeric and celery seed in a saucepan. Bring to a boil. Drain the salty liquid from the vegetables. Pour the spice brine over the vegetables, and let stand for 2 more hours.

Step 3

Bring to a boil once again, and simmer for about 5 minutes. Ladle into 1 pint sterile jars, filling with the liquid to within 1/4 inch of the top. Wipe rims with a clean towel, and run a thin spatula around the inside of the jar to remove air bubbles. Seal with lids and rings. Process for 10 minutes in a simmering water bath to seal completely.

Tips

For safety when canning and preserving foods, contact your local extension for processing times in your area that will be specific to your altitude.

Nutrition Facts

Per Serving:

524.5 calories; protein 3.9g 8% DV; carbohydrates 129.8g 42% DV; fat 1.5g 2% DV; cholesterolmg; sodium 9.1mg.

North Carolina-Style Pulled Pork

Prep: 1 hr **Cook:** 6 hrs **Additional:** 8 hrs **Total:** 15 hrs **Servings:** 10 **Yield:** 10 servings

Ingredients

- 1 tablespoon mild paprika
- 2 teaspoons light brown sugar
- 1 ½ teaspoons hot paprika

- ½ teaspoon celery salt
- ½ teaspoon garlic salt
- ½ teaspoon dry mustard
- ½ teaspoon ground black pepper
- ½ teaspoon onion powder
- ¼ teaspoon salt
- 8 pounds pork butt roast
- 2 cups cider vinegar
- 1 ⅓ cups water
- ⅝ cup ketchup
- ¼ cup firmly packed brown sugar
- 5 teaspoons salt
- 4 teaspoons crushed red pepper flakes
- 1 teaspoon ground black pepper
- 1 teaspoon ground white pepper
- 2 pounds hickory wood chips, soaked

Directions

Step 1

In a small bowl, mix mild paprika, light brown sugar, hot paprika, celery salt, garlic salt, dry mustard, ground black pepper, onion powder, and salt. Rub spice mixture into the roast on all sides. Wrap in plastic wrap, and refrigerate 8 hours, or overnight.

Step 2

Prepare a grill for indirect heat.

Step 3

Sprinkle a handful of soaked wood over coals, or place in the smoker box of a gas grill. Place pork butt roast on the grate over a drip pan. Cover grill, and cook pork until pork is tender and shreds easily, about 6 hours. Check hourly, adding fresh coals and hickory chips as necessary to maintain heat and smoke.

Step 4

Remove pork from heat and place on a cutting board. Allow the meat to cool approximately 15 minutes, then shred into bite-sized pieces using two forks. This requires patience.

Step 5

In a medium bowl, whisk together cider vinegar, water, ketchup, brown sugar, salt, red pepper flakes, black pepper, and white pepper. Continue whisking until brown sugar and salt have dissolved. Place shredded pork and vinegar sauce in a large roasting pan, and stir to coat pork. Serve immediately, or cover and keep warm on the grill for up to one hour until serving.

Nutrition Facts

Per Serving:

425.9 calories; protein 39.1g 78% DV; carbohydrates 12.1g 4% DV; fat 23.1g 36% DV; cholesterol 134.9mg 45% DV; sodium 1698.4mg 68% DV.

Easy Cucumber Salad

Prep: 20 mins **Additional:** 4 hrs **Total:** 4 hrs 20 mins **Servings:** 4 **Yield:** 4 servings

Ingredients

- 2 tablespoons white vinegar
- 1 tablespoon chopped fresh parsley
- 1 tablespoon chopped fresh dill
- 1 teaspoon minced garlic
- 1 tablespoon white sugar
- 1 teaspoon salt
- 1 seedless cucumber, peeled and chopped

Directions

Step 1

Whisk together the vinegar, parsley, dill, garlic, sugar, and salt in a bowl; add the cucumber and stir to coat. Cover and chill in refrigerator 4 to 8 hours. Stir well before serving.

Nutrition Facts

Per Serving:

24.6 calories; protein 0.6g 1% DV; carbohydrates 6g 2% DV; fat 0.1g; cholesterolmg; sodium 584mg 23% DV.

Sauteed Cherry Tomatoes with Garlic and Basil

Servings: 8 **Yield:** 8 servings

Ingredients

- 2 tablespoons olive oil, divided
- 2 pints cherry or grape tomatoes
- 1 pinch Salt and pepper
- 2 garlic clove (blank)s garlic cloves, minced
- 1 tablespoon minced fresh basil

Directions

Step 1

Heat 1 Tb. olive oil in a 12-inch skillet over medium-high flame until it just starts to smoke. Add tomatoes, and season with salt and pepper. Saute, shaking pan frequently, until tomatoes soften and skins just begin to wrinkle, about 2 minutes. Stir in the garlic and continue to shake the pan until garlic is fragrant. Off heat, stir in the basil and remaining 1 Tb. olive oil, then serve.

Nutrition Facts

Per Serving:

46.7 calories; protein 0.7g 1% DV; carbohydrates 3.7g 1% DV; fat 3.6g 6% DV; cholesterolmg; sodium 6.9mg.

Watermelon Agua Fresca

Prep: 25 mins **Total:** 25 mins **Servings:** 8 **Yield:** 8 servings

Ingredients

- 4 cups cubed seeded watermelon
- ½ cup water
- ½ cup white sugar, or to taste
- 4 slices lime
- 24 leaf (blank)s fresh mint leaves
- 1 cup ice

Directions

Step 1

Puree the watermelon and water in a blender until smooth. Add sugar to taste. Cut the lime slices in half. Place a half lime slice into each of 8 glasses along with 3 mint leaves. Crush with a cocktail muddler, then fill each glass with ice. Pour in the watermelon agua fresca, and stir before serving.

Nutrition Facts

Per Serving:

72.4 calories; protein 0.5g 1% DV; carbohydrates 18.7g 6% DV; fat 0.1g; cholesterolmg; sodium 1.3mg.

Tomato, Basil, and Feta Salad

Prep: 15 mins **Total:** 15 mins **Servings:** 4 **Yield:** 4 servings

Ingredients

- 6 plum tomato (blank)s roma (plum) tomatoes, diced
- 1 small cucumber - peeled, quartered lengthwise, and chopped
- 3 medium (4-1/8" long)s green onions, chopped
- ¼ cup fresh basil leaves, cut into thin strips
- 3 tablespoons olive oil
- 2 tablespoons balsamic vinegar
- 3 tablespoons crumbled feta cheese
- 1 pinch salt and freshly ground black pepper to taste

Directions

Step 1

In a large bowl, toss together the tomatoes, cucumber, green onions, basil, olive oil, balsamic vinegar, and feta cheese. Season with salt and pepper.

Nutrition Facts

Per Serving:

140 calories; protein 2.4g 5% DV; carbohydrates 7.4g 2% DV; fat 11.9g 18% DV; cholesterol 6.3mg 2% DV; sodium 88.6mg 4% DV.

Thai Spicy Basil Chicken Fried Rice

Prep: 30 mins **Cook:** 10 mins **Total:** 40 mins **Servings:** 6 **Yield:** 6 servings

Ingredients

- 3 tablespoons oyster sauce
- 2 tablespoons fish sauce
- 1 teaspoon white sugar
- ½ cup peanut oil for frying
- 4 cups cooked jasmine rice, chilled
- 6 large cloves garlic clove, crushed
- 2 peppers serrano peppers, crushed
- 1 pound boneless, skinless chicken breast, cut into thin strips
- 1 red pepper, seeded and thinly sliced
- 1 onion, thinly sliced
- 2 cups sweet Thai basil
- 1 cucumber, sliced
- ½ cup cilantro sprigs

Directions

Step 1

Whisk together the oyster sauce, fish sauce, and sugar in a bowl.

Step 2

Heat the oil in a wok over medium-high heat until the oil begins to smoke. Add the garlic and serrano peppers, stirring quickly. Stir in the chicken, bell pepper, onion and oyster sauce mixture; cook until the chicken is no longer pink. Raise heat to high and stir in the chilled rice; stir quickly until the sauce is blended with the rice. Use the back of a spoon to break up any rice sticking together.

Step 3

Remove from heat and mix in the basil leaves. Garnish with sliced cucumber and cilantro as desired.

Nutrition Facts

Per Serving:

794.1 calories; protein 29.1g 58% DV; carbohydrates 116.4g 38% DV; fat 22.1g 34% DV; cholesterol 46.1mg 15% DV; sodium 469.1mg 19% DV.

Pineapple Coconut Zucchini Bread

Prep: 30 mins **Cook:** 50 mins **Additional:** 2 hrs **Total:** 3 hrs 20 mins **Servings:** 24 **Yield:** 2 - 9x5 inch loaves

Ingredients

- 3 cups all-purpose flour
- 2 teaspoons baking soda
- 1 ½ teaspoons baking powder
- 1 teaspoon salt
- 1 teaspoon ground cinnamon
- 1 teaspoon pumpkin pie spice
- 3 large eggs eggs
- 1 cup vegetable oil
- 1 cup white sugar
- 1 cup light brown sugar
- ½ cup sour cream
- 2 teaspoons vanilla extract
- 3 cups grated unpeeled zucchini
- 1 (20 ounce) can crushed pineapple, well drained
- ½ cup shredded coconut

Directions

Step 1

Preheat oven to 350 degrees F (175 degrees C). Lightly grease two 9x5 inch loaf pans. Stir together flour, baking soda, baking powder, salt, cinnamon, and pumpkin pie spice in a bowl until well blended; set aside.

Step 2

Whisk eggs, oil, white sugar, and brown sugar together in a large bowl. Stir in sour cream, vanilla, zucchini, pineapple, and coconut. Stir in the flour mixture, mixing just until moistened. Divide batter between the prepared loaf pans.

Step 3

Bake until a toothpick inserted in the center comes out clean, 50 to 60 minutes. Cool in pans for 10 minutes, then remove and finish cooling on a wire rack.

Nutrition Facts

Per Serving:

242.5 calories; protein 3g 6% DV; carbohydrates 31.3g 10% DV; fat 12.2g 19% DV; cholesterol 25.4mg 9% DV; sodium 248.1mg 10% DV.

Sean's Falafel and Cucumber Sauce

Prep: 20 mins **Cook:** 10 mins **Additional:** 30 mins **Total:** 1 hr **Servings:** 4 **Yield:** 4 servings

Ingredients

For Sauce:

- 1 (6 ounce) container plain yogurt
- ½ cucumber - peeled, seeded, and finely chopped
- 1 teaspoon dried dill weed
- ½ teaspoon salt and pepper to taste
- 1 tablespoon mayonnaise

For Falafel:

- 1 (15 ounce) can chickpeas (garbanzo beans), drained
- 1 onion, chopped
- ½ cup fresh parsley
- 2 cloves garlic, chopped
- 1 egg
- 2 teaspoons ground cumin
- 1 teaspoon ground coriander
- 1 teaspoon salt
- 1 dash pepper
- 1 pinch cayenne pepper
- 1 teaspoon lemon juice
- 1 teaspoon baking powder
- 1 tablespoon olive oil
- 1 cup dry bread crumbs
- 1 quart oil for frying
- 2 eaches pita breads, cut in half
- 1 cup chopped tomatoes

Directions

Step 1

In a small bowl combine yogurt, cucumber, dill, salt, pepper and mayonnaise and mix well. Chill for at least 30 minutes.

Step 2

In a large bowl mash chickpeas until thick and pasty; don't use a blender, as the consistency will be too thin. In a blender, process onion, parsley and garlic until smooth. Stir into mashed chickpeas.

Step 3

In a small bowl combine egg, cumin, coriander, salt, pepper, cayenne, lemon juice and baking powder. Stir into chickpea mixture along with olive oil. Slowly add bread crumbs until mixture is not sticky but will hold together; add more or less bread crumbs, as needed. Form 8 balls and then flatten into patties.

Step 4

Heat 1 inch of oil in a large skillet over medium-high heat. Fry patties in hot oil until brown on both sides. Serve two falafels in each pita half topped with chopped tomatoes and cucumber sauce.

Nutrition Facts

Per Serving:

586 calories; protein 14.7g 29% DV; carbohydrates 59.5g 19% DV; fat 33.1g 51% DV; cholesterol 50.3mg 17% DV; sodium 1580.1mg 63% DV.

Key Lime Cake III

Servings: 30 **Yield:** 3 - 8 inch round pans

Ingredients

- 1 (18.25 ounce) package lemon cake mix
- 1 ⅓ cups vegetable oil
- 4 large eggs eggs
- 1 (3 ounce) package lime flavored Jell-O® mix
- ¾ cup orange juice
- ½ cup butter
- 1 (8 ounce) package cream cheese
- 3 tablespoons fresh lime juice
- 4 cups confectioners' sugar

Directions

Step 1

Combine cake mix, gelatin mix, oil, eggs and orange juice. Pour into three 8 inch cake pans. Bake according to instructions on box. Allow to cool, then frost.

Step 2

To make the frosting: In a large bowl, beat the butter and cream cheese until light and fluffy. Add lime juice and confectioners sugar. Mix well.

Nutrition Facts

Per Serving:

297.3 calories; protein 2.8g 6% DV; carbohydrates 32g 10% DV; fat 18.2g 28% DV; cholesterol 45.6mg 15% DV; sodium 189.5mg 8% DV.

Chow Chow I

Prep: 45 mins **Cook:** 15 mins **Additional:** 12 hrs **Total:** 13 hrs **Servings:** 96 **Yield:** 96 servings

Ingredients

- 12 ½ pounds green tomatoes, chopped
- 8 large onions, chopped

- 10 medium (blank)s green bell peppers, chopped
- 3 teaspoons salt
- 6 peppers chopped green chile peppers
- 1 quart distilled white vinegar
- 1 ¾ cups white sugar
- ½ cup prepared horseradish
- 1 tablespoon ground cinnamon
- 1 tablespoon ground allspice
- ¼ teaspoon ground cloves

Directions

Step 1

In a large bowl combine tomatoes, onions, bell peppers and salt. Let stand overnight.

Step 2

Drain the tomato/pepper mixture and add the hot chile peppers, vinegar, sugar, and horseradish. Wrap the cinnamon, allspice, and cloves in cheesecloth or a porous bag, and add to tomato/pepper mixture.

Step 3

Boil for 15 minutes, or until tender.

Step 4

Pack tightly in sterilized jars and seal.

Nutrition Facts

Per Serving:

35.5 calories; protein 0.9g 2% DV; carbohydrates 8.5g 3% DV; fat 0.1g; cholesterolmg; sodium 282.2mg 11% DV.

White Peach Sangria

Prep: 10 mins **Additional:** 2 hrs **Total:** 2 hrs 10 mins **Servings:** 6 **Yield:** 6 servings

Ingredients

- 1 (750 milliliter) bottle dry white wine
- ¾ cup peach flavored vodka
- 6 tablespoons frozen lemonade concentrate, thawed
- ¼ cup white sugar
- 1 pound white peaches, pitted and sliced
- ¾ cup seedless red grapes, halved
- ¾ cup seedless green grapes, halved

Directions

Step 1

In a large pitcher, combine dry white wine, peach vodka, lemonade concentrate and sugar. Stir until sugar is dissolved. Add sliced peaches, red and green grapes.

Step 2

Refrigerate sangria until well chilled, at least 2 hours, or overnight to blend flavors. Serve over ice, and use a slotted spoon to include sliced peaches and grapes with each serving.

Cook's Notes:

I use a fume blanc or sauvignon blanc. You may also use frozen peach slices.

Nutrition Facts

Per Serving:

291 calories; protein 1.1g 2% DV; carbohydrates 34.5g 11% DV; fat 0.5g 1% DV; cholesterolmg; sodium 7.8mg.

Margaritas on the Rocks

Prep: 10 mins **Total:** 10 mins **Servings:** 8 **Yield:** 8 servings

Ingredients

- 2 cups sweet and sour mix
- 1 cup triple sec
- 1 ½ cups gold tequila
- ⅓ cup brandy-based orange liqueur (such as Grand Marnier®)
- 2 lime (2" dia)s limes, quartered

Directions

Step 1

Salt the rims of 8 glasses. To do so, pour salt onto a small plate, rub the rims of the glasses with lime, and press them into the salt. Fill the glasses with ice.

Step 2

In a blender, combine sweet and sour mix, triple sec, tequila and Grand Marnier. Blend until smooth. Pour into glasses, squeeze a quarter lime into each glass, and serve.

Nutrition Facts

Per Serving:

369.1 calories; protein 0.1g; carbohydrates 44g 15% DV; fat 0.2g; cholesterolmg; sodium 3.4mg.

Fried Green Tomatoes

Prep: 10 mins **Cook:** 10 mins **Total:** 20 mins **Servings:** 6 **Yield:** 6 servings

Ingredients

- 1 cup all-purpose flour
- 1 teaspoon salt

- 1 teaspoon pepper
- 5 medium (blank)s green tomatoes, sliced 1/2 inch thick
- 1 cup crushed saltine crackers
- 2 large eggs eggs, beaten
- ½ cup butter

Directions

Step 1

In a small bowl, stir together the flour, salt and pepper. Place the crushed saltine crackers in another bowl, and the beaten eggs in a third bowl.

Step 2

Melt the butter in a large skillet over medium heat. Dip each tomato slice in the egg to coat, then in the flour mixture. Dip the floured tomato slice back into the egg, and then into the cracker crumbs. Place the coated tomato slices in the hot skillet, and fry until golden brown on each side, about 3 to 5 minutes per side. Add more butter to the pan, if necessary. Serve hot!

Nutrition Facts

Per Serving:

309.7 calories; protein 6.8g 14% DV; carbohydrates 29.8g 10% DV; fat 18.7g 29% DV; cholesterol 102.7mg 34% DV; sodium 658.8mg 26% DV.

Peach Upside Down Cake I

Prep: 20 mins **Cook:** 35 mins **Additional:** 5 mins **Total:** 1 hr **Servings:** 9 **Yield:** 8 inch square cake

Ingredients

- ¼ cup butter
- ½ cup packed light brown sugar
- ¼ teaspoon ground nutmeg
- 5 medium (2-1/2" dia) (approx 4 per lb)s fresh peaches - peeled, pitted and halved
- ½ cup butter, softened
- ½ cup white sugar
- 1 egg
- 1 ¼ cups all-purpose flour
- 2 teaspoons baking powder
- ½ teaspoon salt
- ½ cup milk

Directions

Step 1

Preheat oven to 375 degrees F (190 degrees C).

Step 2

Melt 1/4 cup butter or margarine in an 8-inch square pan. Sprinkle with brown sugar and nutmeg. Arrange peach halves, cut side down, in pan.

Step 3

In a large bowl, cream the butter and sugar until light and fluffy. Beat in egg. Stir together flour, baking powder and salt. Add flour mixture to creamed mixture alternately with milk, beating well after each addition. Spread batter over peaches.

Step 4

Bake in preheated oven until lightly browned on top, 35 to 40 minutes. Remove cake from oven, and let stand in pan for 5 minutes; invert onto serving platter.

Nutrition Facts

Per Serving:

317.7 calories; protein 3.1g 6% DV; carbohydrates 40.7g 13% DV; fat 16.4g 25% DV; cholesterol 62.4mg 21% DV; sodium 365.8mg 15% DV.

Simple Cucumber Soup

Prep: 15 mins **Cook:** 25 mins **Total:** 40 mins **Servings:** 3 **Yield:** 3 servings

Ingredients

- 1 tablespoon butter, or more to taste
- 1 tablespoon olive oil
- 1 small yellow onion, chopped
- 1 large clove garlic, minced
- 2 large English cucumbers, peeled and thinly sliced
- 2 small zucchinis, peeled and thinly sliced
- 3 cups vegetable broth

Directions

Step 1

Melt butter with the oil in a large saucepan over medium-high heat. Cook and stir onion and garlic in the butter mixture until tender, 3 to 5 minutes. Add cucumber and zucchini slices; cook and stir until softened, 2 to 3 minutes. Pour vegetable broth over the mixture; bring to a boil, reduce heat to medium-low, and let simmer until the vegetables are cooked through, 20 to 25 minutes. Remove from heat and cool a few minutes.

Step 2

Pour soup into a blender no more than half full. Cover and hold lid in place with a towel; pulse a few times before leaving on to blend. Puree in batches until smooth.

Nutrition Facts

Per Serving:

150.5 calories; protein 3.4g 7% DV; carbohydrates 15g 5% DV; fat 9.3g 14% DV; cholesterol 10.2mg 3% DV; sodium 500.2mg 20% DV.

Garlic Chicken Fried Brown Rice

Prep: 20 mins **Cook:** 15 mins **Total:** 35 mins **Servings:** 3 **Yield:** 3 servings

Ingredients

- 2 tablespoons vegetable oil, divided
- 8 ounces skinless, boneless chicken breast, cut into strips
- ½ red bell pepper, chopped
- ½ cup green onion, chopped
- 4 cloves garlic, minced
- 3 cups cooked brown rice
- 2 tablespoons light soy sauce
- 1 tablespoon rice vinegar
- 1 cup frozen peas, thawed

Directions

Step 1

Heat 1 tablespoon of vegetable oil in a large skillet set over medium heat. Add the chicken, bell pepper, green onion and garlic. Cook and stir until the chicken is cooked through, about 5 minutes. Remove the chicken to a plate and keep warm.

Step 2

Heat the remaining tablespoon of oil in the same skillet over medium-high heat. Add the rice; cook and stir to heat through. Stir in the soy sauce, rice vinegar and peas, and continue to cook for 1 minute. Return the chicken mixture to the skillet and stir to blend with the rice and heat through before serving.

Nutrition Facts

Per Serving:

444.4 calories; protein 24.3g 49% DV; carbohydrates 57.4g 19% DV; fat 12.8g 20% DV; cholesterol 43.1mg 14% DV; sodium 701.4mg 28% DV.

Hawaiian Chicken Kabobs

Prep: 10 mins **Cook:** 20 mins **Additional:** 2 hrs **Total:** 2 hrs 30 mins **Servings:** 8 **Yield:** 8 servings

Ingredients

- 3 tablespoons soy sauce
- 3 tablespoons brown sugar
- 2 tablespoons sherry
- 1 tablespoon sesame oil

- ¼ teaspoon ground ginger
- ¼ teaspoon garlic powder
- 8 breast half, bone and skin removed (blank)s skinless, boneless chicken breast halves - cut into 2 inch pieces
- 1 (20 ounce) can pineapple chunks, drained
- 4 eaches skewers

Directions

Step 1

In a shallow glass dish, mix the soy sauce, brown sugar, sherry, sesame oil, ginger, and garlic powder. Stir the chicken pieces and pineapple into the marinade until well coated. Cover, and marinate in the refrigerator at least 2 hours.

Step 2

Preheat grill to medium-high heat.

Step 3

Lightly oil the grill grate. Thread chicken and pineapple alternately onto skewers. Grill 15 to 20 minutes, turning occasionally, or until chicken juices run clear.

Nutrition Facts

Per Serving:

202.9 calories; protein 23.6g 47% DV; carbohydrates 17.1g 6% DV; fat 4.2g 6% DV; cholesterol 60.8mg 20% DV; sodium 412.6mg 17% DV.

Summer Zucchini Casserole

Prep: 20 mins **Cook:** 35 mins **Total:** 55 mins **Servings:** 4 **Yield:** 4 servings

Ingredients

- 2 pounds sliced zucchini
- ¼ cup chopped onion
- 1 (10.75 ounce) can condensed cream of chicken soup
- 1 cup sour cream
- 1 cup grated carrots
- 1 stick unsalted butter, melted
- 1 (6 ounce) package chicken-flavored dry bread stuffing mix

Directions

Step 1

Preheat oven to 350 degrees F (175 degrees C).

Step 2

Boil the zucchini and onion in water for 5 minutes; drain well. In a medium bowl, combine the soup, sour cream and carrots. Stir in the zucchini and onion and mix well.

Step 3

In a separate medium bowl, combine the butter and stuffing mix. Spread half of this mixture into the bottom of a 9x13-inch baking dish. Spoon the zucchini mixture over the stuffing, then top off with the other half of the stuffing.

Step 4

Bake at 350 degrees F (175 degrees C) for 25 to 30 minutes, or until stuffing is golden brown.

Nutrition Facts

Per Serving:

610.6 calories; protein 11.7g 23% DV; carbohydrates 51.5g 17% DV; fat 41.4g 64% DV; cholesterol 92.8mg 31% DV; sodium 1250.9mg 50% DV.

Greek Garbanzo Bean Salad

Prep: 10 mins **Additional:** 2 hrs **Total:** 2 hrs 10 mins **Servings:** 8 **Yield:** 8 servings

Ingredients

- 2 (15 ounce) cans garbanzo beans, drained
- 2 medium (blank)s cucumbers, halved lengthwise and sliced
- 12 eaches cherry tomatoes, halved
- ½ red onion, chopped
- 2 cloves garlic, minced
- 1 (15 ounce) can black olives, drained and chopped
- 1 ounce crumbled feta cheese
- ½ cup Italian-style salad dressing
- ½ lemon, juiced
- ½ teaspoon garlic salt
- ½ teaspoon ground black pepper

Directions

Step 1

Combine the beans, cucumbers, tomatoes, red onion, garlic, olives, cheese, salad dressing, lemon juice, garlic salt and pepper. Toss together and refrigerate 2 hours before serving. Serve chilled.

Nutrition Facts

Per Serving:

214.3 calories; protein 5.2g 11% DV; carbohydrates 25.5g 8% DV; fat 11.5g 18% DV; cholesterol 3.2mg 1% DV; sodium 1066.8mg 43% DV.

Tomato Bacon Grilled Cheese

Servings: 4 **Yield:** 4 servings

Ingredients

- 8 slices bacon
- ¼ cup butter, softened
- 8 slices white bread
- 8 slices American cheese
- 8 slices tomato

Directions

Step 1

Place bacon in a large, deep skillet. Cook over medium high heat until evenly brown. Drain, and set aside.

Step 2

Heat a large skillet over medium heat. Spread butter onto one side of each slice of bread. Lay 4 slices of bread, butter side down, in the skillet. Top with a slice of cheese, 2 slices tomato, bacon, and another slice of cheese. Cover with a slice of bread, butter side out. Fry sandwiches until golden on both sides.

Nutrition Facts

Per Serving:

557 calories; protein 23.8g 48% DV; carbohydrates 28.6g 9% DV; fat 38.7g 60% DV; cholesterol 104.1mg 35% DV; sodium 1696.1mg 68% DV.

Microwave Bread and Butter Pickles

Prep: 20 mins **Cook:** 10 mins **Total:** 30 mins **Servings:** 24 **Yield:** 3 cups

Ingredients

- 1 large cucumber, sliced
- 1 teaspoon salt
- 1 onion, thinly sliced
- ½ teaspoon mustard seeds
- 1 cup white sugar
- ½ cup distilled white vinegar
- ¼ teaspoon celery seed
- ¼ teaspoon ground turmeric

Directions

Step 1

In a medium microwave safe bowl, mix cucumber, salt, onion, mustard seeds, white sugar, distilled white vinegar, celery seed and turmeric.

Step 2

Microwave on high 7 to 8 minutes, stirring twice, until cucumbers are tender and onion is translucent.

Step 3

Transfer to sterile containers. Seal and chill in the refrigerator until serving.

Nutrition Facts

Per Serving:

36.5 calories; protein 0.2g; carbohydrates 9.2g 3% DV; fatg; cholesterolmg; sodium 97.4mg 4% DV.

Thai Beef Salad

Prep: 30 mins **Cook:** 15 mins **Additional:** 3 hrs **Total:** 3 hrs 45 mins **Servings:** 6 **Yield:** 4 to 6 servings

Ingredients

- 2 medium (4-1/8" long)s green onions, chopped
- 1 lemon grass, cut into 1 inch pieces
- 1 cup chopped fresh cilantro
- 1 cup chopped fresh mint leaves
- 1 cup lime juice
- ⅓ cup fish sauce
- 1 tablespoon sweet chili sauce
- ½ cup white sugar
- 1 ½ pounds (1 inch thick) steak fillet
- 1 head leaf lettuce - rinsed, dried and torn into bite-size pieces
- ½ English cucumber, diced
- 1 pint cherry tomatoes

Directions

Step 1

In a large bowl, stir together the green onions, lemon grass, cilantro, mint leaves, lime juice, fish sauce, chili sauce and sugar until well combined and the sugar is dissolved. Adjust the flavor, if desired, by adding more sugar and/or fish sauce. Set aside.

Step 2

Cook the steak over high heat on a preheated grill for approximately 4-6 minutes on each side, until it is cooked medium. Do not overcook the meat! Remove from heat and slice into thin strips. Add the meat and its juices to the sauce and refrigerate, tightly covered, for at least 3 hours.

Step 3

Tear the lettuce into bite size pieces and place in a salad bowl. Arrange the cucumber on top of the lettuce, and then pour the meat and sauce over. Top with the cherry tomatoes and garnish with fresh cilantro leaves.

Nutrition Facts

Per Serving:

210.8 calories; protein 16g 32% DV; carbohydrates 27.4g 9% DV; fat 5g 8% DV; cholesterol 25.2mg 8% DV; sodium 1050.6mg 42% DV.

Cherry Pepper Poppers

Prep: 25 mins **Additional:** 1 hr **Total:** 1 hr 25 mins **Servings:** 12 **Yield:** 12 stuffed peppers

Ingredients

- 1 cup extra virgin olive oil
- 12 peppers fresh cherry peppers
- 6 ounces sharp provolone cheese, cubed
- 6 ounces prosciutto, thinly sliced
- 1 teaspoon salt

Directions

Step 1

Slice the tops off of the cherry peppers and carefully remove the seeds, keeping peppers whole. Wrap a cube of cheese with prosciutto, and stuff into a pepper. If there is still room inside the pepper, stuff in more prosciutto. Repeat with remaining peppers.

Step 2

Place all of the stuffed peppers into a 1 quart jar - or one that your peppers will all fit into, and sprinkle salt over them. Pour in enough olive oil to cover the peppers. Cover, and let stand for 1 hour before eating. Refrigerate leftovers.

Nutrition Facts

Per Serving:

278 calories; protein 6.6g 13% DV; carbohydrates 2.1g 1% DV; fat 27g 42% DV; cholesterol 22.3mg 7% DV; sodium 592.6mg 24% DV.

Roasted Garlic Zucchini and Tomatoes

Prep: 15 mins **Cook:** 18 mins **Total:** 33 mins **Servings:** 4 **Yield:** 4 servings

Ingredients

- 2 eaches zucchini cut in half lengthwise, then cut into 1/2-inch half moons
- 2 cups quartered ripe tomatoes
- ½ onion, minced
- 3 cloves garlic, minced
- ½ teaspoon crushed red pepper flakes
- ¼ cup olive oil
- 1 pinch salt and pepper to taste
- ½ cup grated Parmesan cheese
- 1 tablespoon chopped fresh basil

Directions

Step 1

Preheat oven to 450 degrees F (230 degrees C). Lightly grease a 9x13 inch baking dish.

Step 2

Combine the zucchini, tomatoes, onion, garlic, and red pepper flakes in the prepared baking dish. Drizzle with the olive oil, season with salt and pepper, and mix well.

Step 3

Place in preheated oven. Roast until vegetables are tender and slightly golden, about 18 minutes. Remove from oven; sprinkle with the Parmesan cheese and basil.

Nutrition Facts

Per Serving:

204.1 calories; protein 5.9g 12% DV; carbohydrates 9.5g 3% DV; fat 16.8g 26% DV; cholesterol 8.8mg 3% DV; sodium 165.2mg 7% DV.

Jersey Fresh Stewed Tomatoes

Prep: 20 mins **Cook:** 20 mins **Total:** 40 mins **Servings:** 8 **Yield:** 8 servings

Ingredients

- 6 large tomatoes - peeled, cored, and chopped
- ¾ cup chopped green bell pepper
- ½ cup chopped sweet onion
- ½ cup chopped celery
- 1 teaspoon white sugar
- ½ teaspoon salt
- ¼ teaspoon dried oregano
- ¼ teaspoon dried basil
- ⅛ teaspoon black pepper
- 1 tablespoon water
- 1 ½ teaspoons cornstarch

Directions

Step 1

Combine tomatoes, green bell pepper, onion, and celery in a large skillet over medium heat; cook and stir until fragrant, about 10 minutes. Reduce heat and cook until green bell pepper and onion are soft, about 5 minutes more. Stir in sugar, salt, oregano, basil, and pepper.

Step 2

Whisk water and cornstarch together in a small bowl. Stir into the skillet. Simmer tomato mixture until thickened, about 5 minutes.

Nutrition Facts

37 calories; protein 1.5g 3% DV; carbohydrates 8.2g 3% DV; fat 0.3g 1% DV; cholesterolmg; sodium 159.1mg 6% DV.

Zucchini Bars

Prep: 15 mins **Cook:** 25 mins **Additional:** 20 mins **Total:** 1 hr **Servings:** 12 **Yield:** 1 9x13-inch pan

Ingredients

- 3 large eggs eggs
- 1 cup vegetable oil
- 2 cups white sugar
- 2 teaspoons vanilla extract
- 2 ⅓ cups all-purpose flour
- ¼ teaspoon baking powder
- 2 teaspoons baking soda
- 1 teaspoon salt
- 2 cups grated zucchini
- ½ cup margarine
- 1 (3 ounce) package cream cheese, room temperature
- 2 ½ cups confectioners' sugar, sifted

Directions

Step 1

Preheat oven to 350 degrees F (175 degrees C). Grease a 9x13 inch pan.

Step 2

In a large bowl, mix together the eggs, oil, sugar and vanilla until well blended. Combine the flour, baking powder, baking soda and salt; stir into the sugar mixture. Mix in the zucchini. Spread the batter evenly into the prepared pan.

Step 3

Bake in preheated oven until a toothpick inserted into the center comes out clean, 20 to 25 minutes.

Step 4

To make the frosting, blend together the margarine, cream cheese and confectioners' sugar until smooth. Spread over warm cake. Allow cake to cool completely before cutting into bars.

Nutrition Facts

Per Serving:

590.1 calories; protein 5g 10% DV; carbohydrates 77.9g 25% DV; fat 29.7g 46% DV; cholesterol 54.3mg 18% DV; sodium 540mg 22% DV.

Easy Garlic Escargots

Prep: 15 mins **Cook:** 25 mins **Additional:** 5 mins **Total:** 45 mins **Servings:** 20 **Yield:** 20 stuffed mushrooms

Ingredients

- 1 (7 ounce) can escargots, drained
- 6 tablespoons butter
- 1 clove garlic, minced
- 20 medium (blank)s mushrooms, stems removed
- ⅓ cup white wine
- ⅓ cup cream
- 1 tablespoon all-purpose flour
- 1 pinch ground black pepper to taste
- ¼ teaspoon dried tarragon
- ¼ cup grated Parmesan cheese

Directions

Step 1

Place escargots in a small bowl, and cover with cold water; set aside for 5 minutes. This will help to remove the canned flavor they may have.

Step 2

Preheat oven to 350 degrees F (175 degrees C). Lightly grease an 8x8 inch baking dish.

Step 3

Drain the water from the escargots and pat dry with a paper towel. Melt butter with the garlic in a large skillet over medium-high heat. Add the escargots and mushroom caps; cook and stir until the mushroom caps begin to soften, about 5 minutes.

Step 4

Whisk together wine, cream, flour, pepper, and tarragon in a small bowl until the flour is no longer lumpy. Pour this into the skillet, and bring to a boil. Cook, stirring occasionally until the sauce thickens, about 10 minutes.

Step 5

Remove the skillet from the heat, and use a spoon to place the mushrooms upside down into the prepared baking dish. Spoon an escargot into each mushroom cap. Pour the remaining sauce over the mushroom caps and into the baking dish. Sprinkle grated Parmesan cheese overtop.

Step 6

Bake in preheated oven until the Parmesan cheese has turned golden brown, 10 to 15 minutes.

Nutrition Facts
Per Serving:

86 calories; protein 5.9g 12% DV; carbohydrates 2.8g 1% DV; fat 5.4g 8% DV; cholesterol 28.6mg 10% DV; sodium 81.1mg 3% DV.

Shoepeg Corn Salad

Prep: 15 mins **Additional:** 2 hrs **Total:** 2 hrs 15 mins **Servings:** 8 **Yield:** 8 servings

Ingredients
Dressing:
- ½ cup mayonnaise
- 3 small green onions, thinly sliced
- 2 tablespoons white wine vinegar
- 2 tablespoons minced pickled jalapeno peppers
- 2 tablespoons minced fresh parsley
- 1 tablespoon light olive oil
- 1 pinch salt and ground black pepper to taste

Vegetables:
- 2 (11 ounce) cans shoepeg corn, rinsed and drained
- 1 cup halved grape tomatoes

Directions
Step 1
Whisk mayonnaise, green onions, vinegar, jalapeno peppers, parsley, and olive oil together in a bowl until smooth; season with salt and pepper.

Step 2
Gently stir corn and tomatoes into the dressing to coat. Transfer salad to a serving dish, cover with plastic wrap, and refrigerate at least 2 hours.

Cook's Note:
Instead of the green onions you can use red onion, diced small and rinsed well under cold water, then patted dry.

Nutrition Facts
Per Serving:
201.1 calories; protein 2.4g 5% DV; carbohydrates 18g 6% DV; fat 13.3g 20% DV; cholesterol 5.2mg 2% DV; sodium 340mg 14% DV.

BBQ Teriyaki Pork Kabobs

Prep: 30 mins **Cook:** 20 mins **Additional:** 3 hrs **Total:** 3 hrs 50 mins **Servings:** 6 **Yield:** 6 servings

Ingredients
- 3 tablespoons soy sauce

- 3 tablespoons olive oil
- 1 clove garlic, minced
- ½ teaspoon crushed red pepper flakes
- ⅛ teaspoon salt and pepper to taste
- 1 pound boneless pork loin, cut into 1 inch cubes
- 1 (14.5 ounce) can low-sodium beef broth
- 2 tablespoons cornstarch
- 2 tablespoons soy sauce
- 1 tablespoon brown sugar
- 2 cloves garlic, minced
- ¼ teaspoon ground ginger
- 3 mushrooms portobello mushrooms, cut into quarters
- 1 large red onion, cut into 12 wedges
- 12 eaches cherry tomatoes
- 12 bite-size chunks fresh pineapple

Directions

Step 1

In a shallow dish, mix together 3 tablespoons soy sauce, olive oil, 1 clove minced garlic, red pepper flakes, salt, and pepper. Add pork cubes, and turn to coat evenly with marinade. Cover, and refrigerate for 3 hours.

Step 2

In a saucepan, combine beef broth, cornstarch, 2 tablespoons soy sauce, brown sugar, 2 cloves minced garlic, and ginger. Bring to a boil, stirring constantly. Reduce heat, and simmer 5 minutes.

Step 3

Preheat an outdoor grill for high heat and lightly oil grate. Thread pork cubes onto skewers, alternating with mushrooms, onion, tomatoes, and pineapple chunks.

Step 4

Cook on grill for 15 minutes, or until meat is cooked through. Turn skewers, and baste often with sauce during cooking.

Nutrition Facts

Per Serving:

297 calories; protein 19.4g 39% DV; carbohydrates 17.6g 6% DV; fat 17g 26% DV; cholesterol 47.6mg 16% DV; sodium 867.2mg 35% DV.

Maria's Pepper Steak

Prep: 20 mins **Cook:** 30 mins **Total:** 50 mins **Servings:** 4 **Yield:** 4 servings

Ingredients

- 2 tablespoons olive oil

- 1 medium onion, chopped
- 2 large bell peppers, sliced into thin strips
- 2 cloves garlic, minced
- ⅓ cup soy sauce
- ⅓ cup honey
- ⅓ cup red wine vinegar
- 1 ½ pounds flank steak, cut into thin strips

Directions

Step 1

Heat olive oil in a skillet over medium heat. Cook onion, bell peppers, and garlic in oil until tender-crisp, stirring frequently. Set aside.

Step 2

Heat a large skillet over medium-high heat. Pour soy sauce, honey, and red wine vinegar in pan, then add beef. Cook beef, stirring frequently, until done, about 10 to 15 minutes. Stir in cooked vegetables, and cook another 10 to 15 minutes.

Note

If you prefer a thicker sauce, stir in a little flour or corn starch before removing from heat.

Nutrition Facts

Per Serving:

387.5 calories; protein 22.6g 45% DV; carbohydrates 33g 11% DV; fat 19.2g 30% DV; cholesterol 53.6mg 18% DV; sodium 1259.5mg 50% DV.

Mama's Blackberry Cobbler

Prep: 10 mins **Cook:** 45 mins **Total:** 55 mins **Servings:** 9 **Yield:** 1 8x8-inch pan

Ingredients

- ½ cup butter, melted
- 1 cup white sugar
- 1 cup self-rising flour
- ¾ cup milk
- 2 cups fresh blackberries

Directions

Step 1

Preheat oven to 350 degrees F (175 degrees C).

Step 2

Pour the melted butter into the bottom of an 8x8-inch square baking pan. Mix the sugar, self-rising flour, and milk together until moistened, and pour the mixture over the butter. Do not stir. Spread blackberries evenly over the batter.

Step 3

Bake in the preheated oven until the top is browned and the cobbler is bubbling, about 45 minutes.

Nutrition Facts

Per Serving:

249.5 calories; protein 2.6g 5% DV; carbohydrates 36.6g 12% DV; fat 10.9g 17% DV; cholesterol 28.7mg 10% DV; sodium 257.7mg 10% DV.

Hot Pepper Sauce - A Trinidadian Staple

Prep: 30 mins **Total:** 30 mins **Servings:** 100 **Yield:** 3 cups

Ingredients

- 15 peppers habanero peppers
- 1 small mango - peeled, seeded, and cut into chunks
- 1 onion, roughly chopped
- 3 medium (4-1/8" long)s green onions, roughly chopped
- 2 cloves garlic, roughly chopped
- 1 ½ cups distilled white vinegar
- 2 lime (2" dia)s limes, juiced
- 2 tablespoons vegetable oil
- 4 tablespoons dry mustard powder
- 1 tablespoon salt
- 1 teaspoon curry powder
- ½ teaspoon grated lime zest

Directions

Step 1

Wearing disposable gloves, and being careful not to get any in your eyes or on your skin, roughly chop the habanero peppers. Place the habanero peppers, mango, onion, green onions, and garlic into a blender. Pour in the vinegar, lime juice, and vegetable oil, cover the blender, and pulse until the mixture is very finely chopped. Stop the blender, and add dry mustard powder, salt, curry powder, and lime zest. Blend again until the sauce is smooth. Pour into clean jars, and store in refrigerator.

Nutrition Facts

Per Serving:

7.1 calories; protein 0.2g; carbohydrates 0.7g; fat 0.4g 1% DV; cholesterolmg; sodium 70.1mg 3% DV.

Raspberry Jalapeno Jelly

Prep: 20 mins **Cook:** 10 mins **Total:** 30 mins **Servings:** 32 **Yield:** 1 pint

Ingredients

- 1 cup fresh or frozen raspberries
- ½ cup chopped green bell pepper
- ¼ cup chopped jalapeno pepper
- 3 cups white sugar
- ¾ cup apple cider vinegar
- ⅓ (6 fluid ounce) container liquid pectin
- 1 sprig fresh mint

Directions

Step 1

Sterilize jars and lids by immersing in boiling water for at least 5 minutes.

Step 2

In a saucepan, combine the raspberries, bell pepper, and jalapeno peppers with the sugar and cider vinegar. Bring to a boil over medium-high heat, and boil rapidly for 1 minute. Remove from heat and let stand for 5 minutes.

Step 3

Stir in the liquid pectin, and run the mixture through a strainer to remove bits of peppers. Pour the strained liquid into sterilized jars, and seal. Store in a cool dark place. Refrigerate after opening.

Nutrition Facts

Per Serving:

76.5 calories; protein 0.1g; carbohydrates 19.5g 6% DV; fatg; cholesterolmg; sodium 0.5mg.

Printed in Great Britain
by Amazon

78873806R00061